SpringerBriefs in Computer Science

More information about this series at http://www.springer.com/series/10028

Felix Mohr

Automated Software and Service Composition

A Survey and Evaluating Review

 Springer

Felix Mohr
Department of Computer Science
Paderborn University
Paderborn
Germany

ISSN 2191-5768   ISSN 2191-5776 (electronic)
SpringerBriefs in Computer Science
ISBN 978-3-319-34167-5   ISBN 978-3-319-34168-2   (eBook)
DOI 10.1007/978-3-319-34168-2

Library of Congress Control Number: 2016939580

Printed on acid-free paper

This Springer imprint is published by Springer Nature
The registered company is Springer International Publishing AG Switzerland

Preface

This book is the result of an exhaustive literature review I carried out in order to determine related work of my Ph.D. thesis.

It was motivated by the difficulty of getting an overview of the field of automated software composition in spite of the numbers of already existing surveys and the unclear search criteria they applied. Reading existing surveys only resulted in a list of approaches with no or only highly superficial discussions on relations among them. However, figuring out these differences and discussing the use cases and usefulness of the approaches is the actual work and the value of a survey. It is the aim of this book to save a great deal of time for those doing research in the area of automated software composition and who seek to locate their work within the pool of hundreds of others with similar (and sometimes even equal) titles but heavily different content.

Having the goal to be as transparent as possible regarding the inclusion and exclusion of papers, this book is accompanied by a web page containing all the papers found in the discourse of the search but finally excluded. Hence, if the reader is missing his approach, he or she is invited to visit the web page, http://felixmohr. eu/research/crc901/survey, where an explanation for the exclusion is given for each identified paper (of the 100.000). Also, if an author finds that the presentation of his approach is not adequate, I would be glad to discuss his or her objections.

There was a discussion on the title of this book during the review process. Initially, this book was entitled "Automated Software Composition." However, most papers discussed in this book treat a problem called service composition, which caused the question: why should it not be entitled "Automated Service Composition". I would argue that service composition *is* software composition (just a new name for the same thing). Of course, there are aspects in services that were not considered before, e.g., quality of service, but it is actually not possible to find a convincing example of software composition that cannot also be posed as a service composition problem. Talks with colleagues, e.g. at ASE 2014, clearly showed that it is important to show service composition in the context of the history of software composition and not as an isolated discipline. It is just that the idea of services revitalized automated software composition and brought its own brand. Even though there are more publications on service composition, they can be located on the research line of traditional software composition. Since many authors are not aware of these roots, I consider it particularly important to also consider non-service composition approaches. Consequently, we decided to change the title to its current form in order to align the reader's supposed expectation with the actual book content.

Finally, I would like to add that this book was created in the context of my research on automated service composition within the Collaborative Research Center "On-The-Fly Computing" (SFB 901); this work, hence, was directly and financially supported by the German Research Foundation (DFG). Within this research project, the reader can find a great deal of interesting publications around (automated) service compositions and research dealing with service composition in on-the-fly service markets, i.e., quality assurance, privacy, service deployment, and much more.

Paderborn   Felix Mohr
February 2016

Contents

Chapter 1
Introduction

The aim of this book is to provide researchers in the area of automated software composition with (i) a complete and comprehensive guide that helps understand the field and easily relate new approaches to existing ones and (ii) literature recommendations for potentially relevant related work. In this book, term "automated software composition" refers to the process of automatically assembling a new software artifact using existing ones.

Automated software composition has been tackled by many people in one way or the other, and it is hard to keep track of the approaches developed so far and to understand important differences among them. For example, in 2009 two algorithms claiming to tackle "the" service composition problem were published with somewhat contradictory evaluation results [14, 23]. On one hand, Bertoli et al. propose an algorithm technique that needs about 70 s to find a composition out of a repository of 18 services [23]. On the other hand, Bartalos et al. present a mechanism that finds a composition in only 5 ms using a repository of 100.000 services [14]. Clearly, the approaches cannot really address the same task, which rises the question of which exactly are the differences between them. Another example is the different understanding of the composition process itself, which is sometimes interleaved with the execution of services and sometimes not. Understanding the differences and advantages of the different approaches is far from trivial, and judging their suitability or relevance for a particular task is just as hard.

There are already dozens of survey papers [17, 18, 21, 46, 48, 49, 80, 96, 101, 114, 120, 130, 142, 147], but these contain merely neutral paper descriptions instead of helpful discussions. Indeed, some of these surveys are worth being read carefully, because they contain a lot of valuable information. My objection is, however, that the reader does not learn anything about the appropriateness of assumptions made by the described approaches, potential use cases, and their scientific quality (formal soundness, evaluation, etc.). For example, several of the above surveys pose Petri nets as a possible model for services. While one *can* model services with Petri nets, other techniques are much more appropriate (cf. Sect. 4.1.2.3); putting the technique on one level with others is irritating to the reader. *Judging* the approaches, which is the actual challenge, is only ever left to the reader; of course, this is usually impossible without

© The Author(s) 2016
F. Mohr, *Automated Software and Service Composition*,
SpringerBriefs in Computer Science, DOI 10.1007/978-3-319-34168-2_1

reading the papers one by one. Also, none of the above surveys can be considered a systematic literature review. That is, the choice of discussed approaches is arbitrary and it is not at all clear why an approach is included or excluded from the overview.

1.1 Contribution and Scope

This book is by far the most exhaustive and systematic review that has been carried out on the field of automated software composition. In order to create this survey, I analyzed many dozens of papers with respect to the concrete problem they tackle and the proposed solutions. This book gives both an overview and a *qualitative comparison* of the approaches.

More precisely, it is a literature review answering three research questions:

1. *Which types of automated software composition problems exist?*
   This question aims at *classifying* the variants of automated software composition problems using the most distinguishing features. It also asks for the *goals and capabilities* inherent to these classes.
2. *Which are the typical use cases where these problems occur?*
   This asks for *situations* in which we would apply the different approaches.
3. *Which are the most prominent solution paradigms for the different types?*
   Here we examine the *solution techniques* used to address the problems.

The first and the second questions are partially answered in Chap. 2. The field of automated software composition can be divided into two areas. Approaches in the first area assume that the behavior of the target software artifact is described by a template that must be instantiated; the main use case is to find an admissible and possibly optimal *refinement of an abstract workflow for an individual context of usage*. Approaches in the second area assume that the behavior is described in terms of logical preconditions and postconditions; the main use case is that we want to *convert a declarative programming statement into imperative code*. Chapter 2 explains why this high-level classification is a good choice and gives answers to the question of use cases for the two classes.

However, the classification system I apply is rather distributed over the three chapters. Chapter 2 explains the two high-level classes, their use cases and differences between them but does not provide a discussion on their respective subclasses. These discussions are part of the introduction of Chap. 3 (for approaches that assume a template given) and Chap. 4 (for approaches that create compositions from scratch) respectively. The reason is that the these classifications are very specific and can be better explained in the respective context. The big picture can be found in Chap. 5; Fig. 5.1 merges these distributed class descriptions into one single classification scheme.

Hence, Chap. 2 should be seen as a general introduction into the field of software composition but without the claim to provide a complete classification framework. The detailed discussion of the two main classes that also contains the answers to the research questions takes place in Chaps. 3 and 4 respectively. The implied merged classification tree can be found in the conclusion in Chap. 5.

For every approach, there is a detailed discussion and a summarizing evaluation comprising strengths and weaknesses. The detail of discussion depends on several factors such as the novelty, quality of the presentation and the used formal model.

However, the reader may also miss two aspects of discussion:

- *Comparison of performance.* I claim that it is not possible to give a comparison of the performance of composition approaches without a centralized challenge. They cannot be compared merely by the results claimed to have been obtained in the respective papers. However, implementations are often not available, and there is no standardized benchmark set for software composition, yet. Hence, a quantitative comparison of approaches would be desirable but is beyond the scope of this book.
- *Comparison of tool support.* The availability of tools is of tremendous importance for the practical relevance of an approach. However, tools with roots in the scientific community often tend to expire. In fact, some of the approaches discussed here such as OWLS-XPlan once came with tools that are not available anymore or only work on outdated platforms. In order to keep the content of this book independent from changes that tend to occur over time, tool support is not part of the comparative discussion.

In the following, I describe how the approaches discussed in this book were determined. That is, the methodology under which the systematic literature review was carried out.

1.2 Method for Selection of Approaches

This section describes how the approaches discussed in this book were identified. Sect. 1.2.1 describes how a basis of approaches was created, and Sect. 1.2.2 describes how the final set was achieved out of these.

1.2.1 Creating a Basis for Selection

1.2.1.1 Initial Set of Potentially Relevant Publications

First, I created an initial set of publications systematically using the scientific search engines Google Scholar, Citeseer, and Science Direct. The search terms used for this process consisted of two words that must be contained in the title of the publications. The first keyword indicates a composition *activity* and the second keyword indicates a *subject* of composition.

The considered keywords for the activity were: composition, compose, composing, composer, synthesis, synthesize, synthesizing, synthesizer, configuration, configure, configuring, configurator, coordination, coordinate, coordinating, coordinator, orchestration, orchestrate, orchestrating, orchestrator, plan, planning, replanning, planner, adapter, adapting, adaption, adapt, connector, connect, connecting, connection, mediator, mediating, mediation, mediate, and choreography.

The considered keywords for the subject were: service, services, component, components, software, program, programs, module, modules, operation, operations, workflow, workflows, process, and processes.

I performed a search for each such combination of keywords. A publication is included if, for at least one search term, it contains all words of the search term in its *title*; this resulted in a basic set of 118.530 publications.

1.2.1.2 Removing Topically False Positives and Manually Excluded

Since keywords may be used in different semantic contexts, there are many approaches with titles that seem relevant to the topic of service composition but which are not. So at this step, I removed approaches that are in no way related to the field of service composition, e.g., biological processes, etc.

This removal was done semiautomatically using stoplists with black listed words that clearly indicate an off-topic publication. The blacklisted words are: biol, biodiv, chemi, molec, toxi, amino, diox, silic, medic, lipid, fischer, family, nano, psychiatric, psycho, physio, lympho, human, pharma, pheromone, cataly, oil, child, adult, hydro, thermal, zeolit, liquid, food, milk, nitro, organ, education, kine, fusion, cultur, acetyl, choline, brain, nerve, magnet, spectr, geom, chlor, amphenicol, dna, gluco, stereos, tumor, cancer, infect, protein, lactam, bacillus, depress, gas, fpga, micro, macro, ethyl, ramoplanin, alamethicin, cedrene, cedrol, ferro, peptide, ligand, pyridin, pyrrolo, mannosid, drug, galact, ribosomal, proteolysis, school, hospital, music, channel, nucl, nickel, crystal, heat, lumber, combustion, octanol, fuel, methan, bismuth, sol–gel, mineral, oxi, polyol, morph, cell, liver, surgery, teeth, tooth, bone, carbid, metabolic, membrane, cardiac, halogen, electr, smok, water, drink, weight, jogg, body, life, clinic, genes, condens, ionic, photo, energ, atmosph, synops, distill, ecosystem, deposition, public, student, pupil, classroom, lecture, freshman, statewide, institutional, writers, grade, demogr, transport, rhetoric, enterprises, glyce, soybean, larva, ß, anoid, legal, judicial, justi, logistics, osmo, schedul, supply, volcan, magma, melt, cognitive, teach, facilit, laser, patient, spatial, qfd, Arabidopsis, economic, business, product, resource, group, team, age, aging, robot, and mechanic.

This list seems quite restrictive and to potentially exclude papers that actually do have to do something with software synthesis. While this objection is generally true, we must keep in mind that an approach is only excluded this way if *all* the related papers contain a blacklisted word. I admit this problem, but a manual revision of over 100.000 papers would have simply not been practical. For the next time, one could apply some machine learning classifier in order to carry out a more sophisticated detection of false positives.

In addition, I manually created a second blacklist of roughly 150 irrelevant publications that are not related to the topic of interest. This step removed a huge set of publications; 56.891 remained in the pool.

1.2.1.3 Merging Publications to Approaches

Since many authors publish multiple papers on the same or very similar approach, I merged publications to *approaches*. In this paper, an approach is simply a set of publications, all of which have the same first author. This way, the 56.891 publications were merged to 42.808 approaches. Like for publications, I created a blacklist of 34 approaches, which were associated with 167 publications. Hence, after this step, there were 56.724 publications defining 42.774 approaches under consideration. A complete version of this set, later denoted as M_0 can found at http://felixmohr.eu/research/crc901/survey.

1.2.1.4 Computing the Citation Graph

The huge set of publications makes it impossible to review each of them, so the only viable strategy is to use an evaluable criterion for automated processing. Even though not perfect, a good criterion for filtering is the number of citations made and obtained by approaches with respect to other approaches in the considered set. To this end, I created a citation graph for approaches. In this graph, there is one node for every approach (56.724 nodes) and one edge between node n and n' if any publication of approach n *is cited by* any publication of approach n'. If there is an edge from n and n' as well as from n' to n, I only selected the citation link where the later cites the earlier approach. Even though this is not a sufficient criterion for acyclicity in general, the resulting citation graph is acyclic with 18.438 links.

1.2.2 Determining the Considered Approaches

1.2.2.1 Determine Recent Relevant Work

Removing approaches that do not cite enough others of the area: Considering the huge number of publications, it is reasonable to first outsort approaches that do not relate themselves to other approaches in the field. In particular, I require that every approach cites at least five other approaches in the set; this means, every approach with input degree at least five in the citation graph. Of course, this also eliminates important early approaches that could not cite five other approaches; I reinclude them in the following step. Quite amazingly, this step reduced the number of approaches by 98 % to a rather manageable number of 733. Note that the high ratio of outsorted papers is not only caused by flawed related work of papers but also by the fact that the set still contained many approaches from foreign topics; since those approaches do not cite software composition approaches, they do not achieve the required number of made citations and are eliminated in this step.

Removing non-recent approaches: For now, we are interested in rather *recent* approaches, which I define as approaches from the last 5 years. Hence, from the remaining 733 approaches, I removed approaches older than 2010, which resulted in another 77 % reduction and a total number of remaining approaches of 168.

Removing recent but not brand new approaches without impact: Somewhat moderately, I required approaches from 2010, 2011, and 2012 to have obtained at least 3, 2, and 1 citations respectively. The computational base here is the output degree in the original citation graph. That is, a link from n to approach n' also counts for n even if n' was removed in the last step. Approaches from 2013, 2014 and 2015 are not excluded. Formally,

$$
M_1^0 = \left\{ x \in M_0 \; \middle| \; \begin{array}{l} -x \text{ cites at least 5 other approaches from } M_0 \text{ and} \\ -\; x \text{ published in 2010 and has at least 3 citations, or} \\ -\; x \text{ published in 2011 and has at least 2 citations, or} \\ -\; x \text{ published in 2012 and has at least 1 citation, or} \\ -\; x \text{ published in 2013, 2014, or 2015} \end{array} \right\}
$$

In our case, this yielded a set with $|M_2^0| = 87$.

1.2.2.2   Determine Very Influential Approaches

Computing most influential approaches. I define the (citation-based) relevance of an approach as a basic (unconditional) value of 1 that is increased by the relevance of approaches that cite it. For the computation of relevance values, we used the formula $f(n) = 1 + \sum_{n'} 5 \cdot \sqrt{f(n')}$, where n' are successors of n in the original citation graph. Using this function f to determine the relevance, I found the intuitively most influential approaches (based on my own research and on the results of other surveys) having the best values in an appropriate order. For the following, I used the 300 approaches with the highest such values. Formally, I define

$$M_2^0 = \{x \in M_0 \mid \text{there are at most 299 other } x' \in M_0 \text{ with } f(x') > f(x)\}$$

1.2.2.3   Reject Approaches that Ignore Very Influential Works

Based on the recent approaches on one hand, and most influential approaches on the other hand, I update the set of recent approaches that do relate themselves to the most influential papers sufficiently. More precisely, I required that a recent approach cites at least 3 of the 200 most influential approaches.

$$M_1^1 = \{x \in M_1^0 \mid x \text{ cites at least 3 elements of } M_2^0\}$$

This step reduced the recent approaches from $|M_0^1| = 87$ to $|M_1^1| = 52$. This tells a lot about the quality of related work of these publications.

1.2.2.4 Determine Somewhat Relevant Approaches

There are a lot of approaches that are important to track the development of an area but that are neither heavily influential nor very recent. In order to include these, I include approaches with at least one citation *obtained* from and five citations *made* on currently considered approaches.

The definition of the set of somewhat relevant approaches is recursive. Let M_3^0 be the label for the set of somewhat relevant approaches and let $M = M_1^1 \cup M_2^0 \cup M_3^0$. Every approach with a publication with at least one citation obtained from approaches in M and 5 citations made on approaches in M is also in M_3^0 (and hence in M). The obtained citation reflects (some) relevance, and the made citations are a necessary condition for reasonable discussion of related work. Formally,

$$M_3^0 = \left\{ x \in M_0 \,\middle|\, \begin{array}{l} -\text{at least one } y \in M_1^1 \cup M_2^0 \cup M_3^0 \text{ cites } x \text{ and} \\ -x \text{ cites five distinct } y_1, y_2, y_3, y_4, y_5 \in M_1^1 \cup M_2^0 \cup M_3^0 \end{array} \right\}$$

We obtain a set of size $|M_3^0| = 172$. Note that M_1^1, M_2^0, and M_3^0 are not generally disjoint. http://felixmohr.eu/research/crc901/survey contains an overview of which approach is contained in which of the sets.

1.2.2.5 The Final Set of Considered Approaches

First, not all of the 300 most influential approaches are really relevant for the discourse, so I only consider those approaches that are cited by at least two other approaches in the set. Most influential approaches not satisfying this condition may have been important but not for the actual discourse of the topic of automated software composition. Formally,

$$M_2^1 = \left\{ x \in M_2^0 \,\middle|\, \text{at least 2 other approaches from } M_1^1 \cup M_2^0 \cup M_3^0 \text{ cite } x \right\}$$

Of the initially 300 approaches, only 135 satisfy this criterion.

Second, I update the set of approaches in M_1^1 and M_3^0 with respect to the related work. Due to the incredible amount of approaches in the area of automated service composition, every "non-ancient" approach in this domain must relate itself to (and therefore cite) at least 5 other (relevant) approaches.

Formally, this yields the following final recursively defined set:

$$M = \left\{ x \mid x \in M_2^1 \text{ or } (x \in M_1^1 \cup M_3^0 \text{ and } x \text{ cites at least 5 items of } M) \right\}$$

The final set M contains 211 approaches, which I examined manually.

1.2.2.6   Individual Revision of Remaining Approaches

In a very laborious revision process, I then outsorted another 105 of the 218 approaches. There were three main reasons for being outsorted manually. First, an approach was outsorted if its publications did not contain any concrete composition technique; these were basically surveys and roadmap papers and papers dealing with nonautomated techniques. Second, an approach was outsorted if it does not discuss related work at all (but merely lists other papers) or does not discuss very relevant related work in sufficient detail; the latter was the case when an approach extends an existing one but does not explain the difference. Third, flaws with respect to the content also led to exclusion; the most frequent cases were the lack of a clear contribution statement or unacceptably heavy formal flaws. There is no point in discussing this in more detail within this paper, but I provide a justification for the exclusion of any manually excluded approach elsewhere.

I acknowledge that this last criterion is, in parts, subjective, but it is still better than previously published surveys. Not only is every survey published so far *completely* based on subjective selection criteria, but these criteria are even nontransparent. The reader has no chance to reconstruct the results and must blindly trust in the quality of research done by the respective authors.

Chapter 2
Automated Software Composition—A Top View

This chapter gives a brief introduction to automated software composition. Section 2.1 provides an overview of the general task of automated software composition. Then, Sect. 2.2 gives an overview over the features of composition problems. Third, Sect. 2.3 proposes *the first level* of a classification scheme, which is the basis for the technical discussions in the next chapters; i.e., it presents the two main classes of composition problems. The discussion of subclasses of the two main classes is part of Chaps. 3 and 4. A summary of the complete classification tree is depicted in Fig. 5.1 in Chap. 5.

2.1 Background

A nice vision statement of automated software composition was given by Koza end Rice in the context of automated programming [76]:

> The goal in automatic programming is to get a computer to perform a task by telling it what needs to be done, rather than by explicitly programming it.

While avoiding explicit programming often is desireable, automated software composition does not aim at replacing classical software development. As pointed out by Hoare, one of the most important properties of software is that "it carries out its intended function" [58]. To express this intended function, we will always need to rely on some kind of formal descriptions, and there is not the illusion of the cocktail party explanation of the vision of automated programming [131], where complex software can be derived from natural language requirement definitions expressed by somebody not even familiar with software engineering. On the other hand, the work of software developers can be *supported* by automation techniques.

The idea of automated software composition is to automate a small part of the code construction process. That is, we do not want to create huge software specifications, press the button, and wait for the signal that the desired software has been deployed on the machine. Instead, we want the machine to create rather simple programs *fast*.

© The Author(s) 2016
F. Mohr, *Automated Software and Service Composition*,
SpringerBriefs in Computer Science, DOI 10.1007/978-3-319-34168-2_2

There seem to be two main cases where automated software composition is preferable over ordinary programming.

First, there may be occasions where we need to create software within the time frame of seconds where any human interaction would simply not be fast enough. For example, we want to run a script that solves an optimization algorithm based on simplex if the instance is rather small and with interior point if it is large, applying specific parameters to the respective algorithm depending on the input instance, which cannot be efficiently hard-coded in the script. We then would create a rough workflow of the general process and automatically refine it at runtime based on the concrete input.

Second, developers often only want to state conditions that should be true for an object instead of describing *how* this is achieved. For example, one would like to be able to write

```
y s.t. PriceOf(y,x) & EUR(y)
```

to say that y should be set to the price of x with respect to its current value in EUR instead of writing the following:

```
p := getBookPriceOf(x);
y = USD2EUR(p);
```

The declarative variant has many advantages. Not only is it closer to the actual intention of the developer, simpler (no temporary variable) and exhibits higher readability. It also decouples description from implementation, which means that the developer does not need to know the exact function that realizes the functionality; the name or location of the function may change without doing harm to the code. In particular, the developer does not even need to know how the property can be computed and whether or not the result is already in the right currency or whether it must be converted. Moreover, given the correctness of the functions used by the synthesizer, the generated code is correct by construction.

The largest subfield of automated software composition is called automated *service* composition. Services are self-contained and platform independent software components. Self-contained means that services do not visibly rely on other components or services, so they can be used right away without the necessity to specify components that should be used for some required interfaces. Platform independent means that two services can be used together independently from the language in which they have been implemented. The idea is that, instead of, say methods in an object oriented programming language, service operations do not communicate by exchanging object references over a commonly accessible memory but by *messages*. These properties allow for the definition of a simple composition model that assumes a set of operations that can be *combined* (platform independentness) ad hoc (self-containedness) into a new software artifact. These properties are naturally given within every programming language, so, by making these assumptions, auto-

mated service composition simply accounts for the fact that we now need to combine
components implemented in possibly different programming languages.

2.2 Features of Software Composition Problems

Clearly, one cannot speak of *the* automated software composition problem. I identified 22 very heterogenous features that separate the service composition problems
from each other. This greate variance makes many approaches distinct and sometimes even completely uncomparable to others. Since most of these features should be
intuitive, I only give a brief overview rather than discussing them in detail. Table 2.1
shows an overview about the features.

Every feature specifies a characteristic that relates to the *algorithm inputs*,
algorithm outputs, or its *behavior*. Composition problems impose conditions on the
inputs, outputs, and even the implementation of composition algorithms (that address
the respective problem). Hence, it is natural to see the set of different features that
determine a composition problem as constraints made on one of these three aspects.

2.2.1 Input Features

The 14 input features describe characteristics about what is fed to a composition
algorithm. Input features are as follows:

- *Presence of a control flow of the solution.*
  In this case, the desired piece of software is specified in form of a workflow, which
  needs to be concretized. The composition algorithm does not create a control flow
  but only refines the given one. Prominent representants where the control flow is
  given are [20, 138, 167], while prominent representants where no control flow is
  specified are [72, 97, 106].
- *Presence of a data flow of the solution.*
  In this case, we already know how data between the potential services will be
  communicated. If the control flow is given, usually also the data flow is given
  or even completely ignored (since not relevant for the composition problem).
  However, it is possible that the data flow is given but the control is not available.
  A prominant approach defined in this setting is the one of Bertoli et al. [23]. The
  task is then to find an admissible *order* of invocations of the services. However,
  most approaches that do not assume the control flow given also assume that no
  data flow is predefined [72, 97, 109].
- *Formalism to describe operation semantics.*
  Not all approaches define the semantics of operations [20, 167]. However, if
  these are specified, this is usually done using logic preconditions and postcon-

Table 2.1 An (uncomplete) overview of features of automated software composition problems and their possible characteristics.

	Feature	Domain (Possible Characteristics of the Respective Feature)
Inputs	Prespecification of Control Flow	not defined, partially or completely defined wrt. structure, semantics, or both
	Prespecification of Data Flow	not defined, partially defined, completely defined
	Operation Descriptions	not specified, explicitly (tags), preconditions & effects
	Language of Descriptions	none, (temporal) propositional logic, arbitrary variants of FOL
	QoS Requirements	none or combination of: hard constraints, soft constraints, objective function
	QoS Ranges	fix values, intervals, distributions
	Input Data	none, example data, target data
	Signature Complexity of Operations	none, at most one input and/or output, arbitrary inputs and outputs
	Deterministic Operation Behavior	no, yes
	Usage Constraints on Operations	no, yes
	Information Gathering versus World Altering	all operations are read-only versus operations also change the state of the world
	Expiration Time of Operation Outputs	invocation and reasonable persistence (IRP) vs. possible invalidation
	General Domain Knowledge	none, taxonomies, ontologies, arbitrary FOL rules
	Object Level Domain Knowledge	not available, available
Outputs	General Type of Output	output is a piece of software, output is the result obtained from *executing* the composition
	Composition Structure	sequences possibly with any combination of: alternatives, loops, flows
	Number of Solutions	one solution, set of solution candidates
	Atomicity of Composition	no, yes (composition can undo steps on failure)
Behavior	Composition & Execution Interleaved	no, yes
	Selection versus Planning	no planning involved, planning involved
	Maximum Usage per Operation	at most once, some upper bound, arbitrary use
	Precondition Satisfaction	preconditions must be satisfied by predecessor, preconditions arbitrarily satisfied

ditions/effects [72, 97, 106] or sometimes through keywords (tags) [99]. I do not consider the usage of (ontological) types as semantic descriptions.

- *Language of semantic descriptions.*
  If operations have descriptions in form of preconditions and effects, these may be specified in different ways. On one hand, they can be propositional, allowing for efficient composition but does not allow to express relations between inputs and outputs of operations [75, 135]. On the other hand, they can be (a subclass of) first order logic [72, 97, 106]. This is significantly more expressive at the natural cost of higher problem complexity.
- *Number of inputs and outputs of operations.*
  Some approaches ignore inputs and outputs completely, since data flow is not important for them [20]. Most other approaches do not impose limitations on the number of inputs and outputs, but it is imaginable to restrict them to only one output (as in Java).
- *How Quality of Service (QoS) is considered.*
  QoS is the common term to describe nonfunctional properties of services. Usually, these are properties like price, throughput, availability, trust, etc. [167]. If considered at all, QoS requirements can be posed as hard constraints [106], soft constraints with penalties [57], or be subject to optimization [167].
- *Description of QoS properties.*
  QoS properties are most of the time considered as scalar values. However, these could be more complex structures such as intervals (value is within a range), density functions (value is a random variable distributed in a particular way), or other functions (e.g., the price of a service depends on the number of invocations within a session).
- *Deterministic behavior of operations.*
  Is the response identical for every two equal invocations? This is the case if the implementation of the operation is stateless and does not contain random elements. Most approaches assume deterministic behavior of operations, but some also consider the more complex case [23].
- *Expiration time of operation outputs and effects.*
  The outputs of an operation invocation usually may become invalid after some time. For example, if the answer is the price of a flight, then the information is only valid within a short range of time. However, most approaches make the assumption of invocation and reasonable persistence (IRP). Under this assumption, the result of an operation invocation remains valid at least throughout the execution of the composition.
- *Information gathering or world altering.*
  If a property P holds after an operation, we must distinguish the case that P was *determined* to hold or whether it was *made* true. Settings that are purely information gathering are read-only settings. Together with the IRP assumption, this means that knowledge gathered by operations does never become false; hence, this constitutes a monotonic setting. In a world altering setting, however, information that was true at some point in the composition may be false later. Every approaches that does

not assume the control flow given implicitly makes this assumption, but, this point is rarely discussed.

- *Dependencies and conflicts among services.*
  Some approaches apply constraints on the common usage of services of the form: If service A is used, then B must not be used.
- *Presence of data to be fed to the solution.*
  Some approaches assume that the data passed to the search composition is already given in the query [98]. This allows for a composition mechanic that interleaves composition and execution. Most approaches, however, do not make this assumption.
- *General domain knowledge is specified.*
  Most approaches only assume a set of services given, but no background knowledge is used [72, 75, 135]. However, there are also some approaches that allow for domain knowledge in form of logic formulas [60,106].
- *Object level domain knowledge.*
  Domain knowledge can be given in form of general rules (previous point) but also in form of facts, e.g., ground literals that are known to be true in a particular domain, e.g., that FRA is an airport close to Frankfurt, Germany. This is particularly relevant in information integration-based settings like [8].

There are very few dependencies among the input features. That is, most combinations of input characteristics is theoretically imaginable. Of course, there are exceptions, e.g., if no QoS requirements are specified, then the ranges of QoS values is irrelevant; or data are only relevant if the operations are considered with inputs and outputs. Still, most features are independent, so I did not present them in form of a (unreasonably dense) feature diagram.

2.2.2 Output Features

I identify four features of the output of the composition algorithm:

- First, a composition algorithm may return a *piece of composed software* or the *result of the execution of a piece of software*. While in the first case the invoker is interested in a functionality that he can reuse arbitrarily often, the second case reflects some kind of database query whose outputs are the results of some more or less complex computation.
- Second, a composition algorithm may return extremely different *composition structures*, which can range from sequences of service operation calls to complex structures with alternative branches, loops, and concurrency.
- Third, a composition algorithm may return *different numbers of solutions*. Since many aspects that may be relevant for the requester cannot be efficiently formalized, the algorithm cannot necessarily take the final decision about the appropriateness of a solution; hence, it may return not only one but a hole set of solution candidates among which the requester can select.

- Finally, compositions may or may not be equipped with the transactional property of *atomicity*, which means that if their execution fails, potentially performed changes on the world are automatically rolled back.

In contrast to the input features, there are some dependencies among these output features. For example, if the general type of the composition output is the result performed by the execution of the identified composition, then the other features are irrelevant. Also, atomicity of compositions somehow requires that the composition is not purely sequential, because purely sequential compositions cannot react on possible execution failures of the invoked operations.

2.2.3 Behavior Features

Finally, I identified four features that describe high level characteristics about the behavior of a composition algorithm.

- First, a composition algorithm may or may not *interleave* the composition process and the software execution process.
- Second, a composition algorithm may be either a pure *selection* algorithm (selects operations for several placeholders of a given template) or a *planning* algorithm (also makes structural decisions on the control flow and data flow). Of course, planning is only relevant if the control flow and data flow are not already completely fixed in the input.
- Third, a composition algorithm may be limited in *how often* it may use (different instances) of every available services and their operations.
- Fourth, planning-based composition algorithms may be limited in *how the preconditions* of added service operations must be satisfied. For example, in [14], the precondition of an operation must be completely satisfied by the immediate predecessor in the control flow.

2.3 The Main Service Composition Problem Classes

In this section, I propose the presence of structural information about the solution as the main criterion for classification. That is, I use only one of the above feature (prespecification of control flow) as a classification criterion. This is a suitable criterion not only because it avoids hybrids that belong into both classes but also because it splits the field into two equally large subfields. This section discusses the goals, main research questions, use cases, and complexity of the two classes.

2.3.1   Class Identification

One way to separate the problems into two intuitive classes is to ask whether or not the structure of the desired composition is given. Here, the term *structure* refers to some form of definition of the control flow of the solution. Figure 2.1 shows this high-level classification scheme. If the structure is given, e.g., in form of a template with placeholders, then the composition problem is to *bind* the placeholders to concrete services. If the structure is not given, then the composition problem is to *find* it, i.e., to find the control and data flow of the desired service.

    Even though other classification criteria are possible, this one is particularly convincing for three reasons. First, it defines a real partition on the field. Either some (possibly partial) structure is available for the input or it is not. For every approach, exactly one of the two assertions is true, so there are no hybrids. Second, the classification separates the field into two roughly equally large subfields, which can be seen in the following two chapters. Third, deciding the class for an approach is easy, because the question whether or not a structure is available can be answered immediately. Consequently, the question whether or not the structure of the solution is known is a good (maybe the best) criterion.

    Another striking argument for this classification is that it distinguishes between two fundamentally different use cases. In the first case, the objective is to find a good *variant* of a known process. In the second case, the objective is to *design* a new process that satisfies a functional requirement specification.

    As a consequence, the motivations and research questions pursued with approaches in the two classes is very different. In the following, I discuss these aspects the goals and the main research questions of the two classes in some more detail. Section 2.3.4 compares the two classes on a high level with each other.

    Since the discussion of subclasses of these two classes is very exhaustive, I defer this discussion to the respective chapters. This is basically because the features used to form the subclasses are different for the two classes. Hence, Chap. 3 discusses the subclasses of the class of approaches that assume that the structure is known,

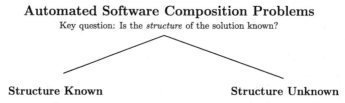

Automated Software Composition Problems

Key question: Is the *structure* of the solution known?

Structure Known	**Structure Unknown**
Situation: The software is already written but contains *placeholders* with fixed semantics that must be bound to concrete pieces of software.	**Situation:** The behavior of the software is described in terms of its *preconditions* and *postconditions*. The structure is unknown or highly abstract.
Goal: Find admissible or optimal binding.	**Goal:** Find control flow and data flow.

Fig. 2.1 The availability of a template is the best classification criterion

and Chap. 4 discusses the subclasses of the class of approaches that assume that the structure is not known. For the same reason, there is not one large decision tree.

2.3.2 Goals and Focus When the Structure is Known

The goal of approaches where the structure of the desired component is known is to construct a machine that refines the abstract description and binds its abstract parts to existing service operations. So the subject of automation is the selection of both an appropriate refinement and the concrete services and operations occuring in them.

The behavior of the desired component is described by a *template*. Figure 2.2 shows a brief sketch of a template and shows that it already specifies the control flow and the data flow (not visualized) of the desired component but leaves placeholders in it, which still must be bound to concrete services. So the eventual composition has already been defined on a more or less abstract level.

Several aspects may play a role in the instantiation process of the predefined template. First, we might consider nonfunctional properties such as price, execution time, etc., and find a solution that is (globally) optimal with respect to these properties. Second, we might consider functional constraints such as the behavior of candidate operations, exclusion constraints, invocation order constraints of used operations, etc. Third, we might be interested in solution that replace placeholders not only by atomic operation calls but by entired subcompositions.

There are several research questions relevant for approaches within this class.

1. How can nonfunctional aspects relevant for service composition be modeled as an optimization problem? Research is mostly concerned about how properties associated with individual service choices must be aggregated to the whole composition.

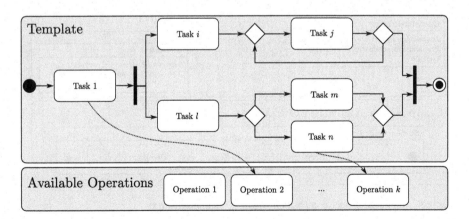

Fig. 2.2 Automated service composition with a given solution structure

2. How can templates be instantiated such that they satisfy functional constraints imposed by the user or the environment? For example, in the Roman model the question is how the placeholders can be replaced such that the communication protocols of used services are satisfied.
3. How can templates be instantiated if placeholders may be bound not only to atomic service operations but to entire compositions that must be created on the fly? Research is mostly concerned with the question how the search process for the instantiation can be designed such that a functionally valid solution is obtained.
4. How can this type of service composition be integrated into the software development workflow?

2.3.3 Goals and Focus When the Structure is Unknown

The goal of approaches that have no structure of the solution given is to construct a machine that computes outputs with the required properties given inputs with the promised properties. Figure 2.3 provides a sketch of this scenario. The intended behavior of the desired composition is specified in terms of *preconditions* that may be assumed to be true on execution and *postconditions* that are expected to hold after execution of the composition.

Approaches in this class devise a new paradigm of programming, which is declarative programming with translation into imperative code before compile time. Instead of writing the code of the desired algorithm itself, i.e., specify functions to be invoked, the developer only says what the algorithm can assume to hold at time of invocation and what should be true at the end of the desired code. Preconditions and postcondi-

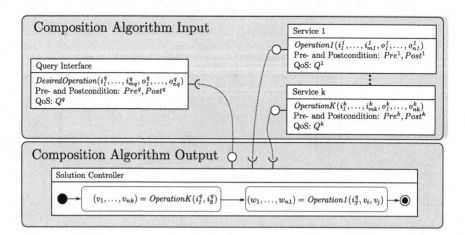

Fig. 2.3 Automated service composition without a solution structure

tions are formulated in terms of propositional or first order logic, sometimes through the notion of ontological concepts.

In other words, approaches in this class aim at exceeding the automation enabled already by compilers for high level languages. In fact, every compiler automatically creates software from a given formal description. However, compilers underly a deterministic translation process, so there is a direct correspondence between what the developer writes and the program that will be created later. Automated software composition goes a step further and allows the developer to use programming constructs that do not even have an executable implementation at design time but whose implementation is tried to be achieved automatically before the compiler is run. In contrast to the translation process of the compiler, which only fails on invalid inputs, the composition process may also fail because it cannot find an implementation with the requested properties.

Readers familiar with verification will notice the close relation between automated service composition and that area. In classical verification, a Hoare triple $\{P\}S\{Q\}$ is correct if we can show that, assuming that the (logical) precondition $\{P\}$ is true, the execution of the code statement S yields the condition $\{Q\}$. Verification assumes the program statement S being given as input for the verification process. In automated software composition, the composition algorithm must *create* a code statement S such that $\{P\}S\{Q\}$ is a correct Hoare triple. Hence, verification is a *subproblem* of this composition problem; usually, it is solved implicitly during search.

There are several research questions related to this composition type.

1. How expressive can (or should) requirements be specified? On one hand, propositional logic is usually not expressive enough, because it cannot relate the outputs produced by an operation to the inputs passed to it. On the other hand, complete first order logic may cause significant computational issues.
2. How can the search process for compositions be designed, and how can it be made efficient? This is simple for many propositional logical requirement definitions but hard for first order logical requirement definitions, (which are of particular interest because of the aforementioned reasons).
3. How can possibly competing nonfunctional properties be considered in this search process?
4. Fourth, how can the acceptance of this very formal approach be increased among developers and how can it be integrated into the development workflow at all?

This is only an (incomplete) overview over the high level questions; of course, each of them can be expanded into many subquestions.

2.3.4 Comparative Discussion of the Classes

The *conceptual* difference between the two classes is not the type of algorithm input but the actual problem that we want to solve. In particular, the two problems have different use cases, are unequally difficult to solve, and are faced with different objections.

Expected Use Cases

In the class of availability of the solution structure, the use case is that we want to find a (possibly optimal) *variant* of a general operation that best suits the individual context and requirements of a *user*. The template contains the algorithm that implements the desired functionality, leaving only some placeholders that may be replaced in different manners depending on the context. This type of composition may be required in situations where different clients want to use the same service but have different preferences regarding nonfunctional properties. For example, both want to use a service that determines the cheapest flights for some journey. While the first client wants the results within a second and accepts a higher price, the second client accepts only a low price but does not care about runtime. The decision how placeholders should be replaced depends on the actual preferences of the requesting client. So the user of the composition algorithm has potentially no or only very few knowledge in the area of software engineering.

The second class corresponds to the use case where a developer wants to have the implementation of an algorithm be generated automatically; the focus is the implementation of some desired *functionality*. This is sometimes called *automated programming*, but a better term would be *code deduction*. The desired functionality has not yet been fixed in a template but must be formulated by the user himself. This can only be done by someone with sufficient skills in software engineering. Hence, the context of this type of composition is a software development environment that combines imperative or functional programming with this type of code deduction.

Unequal Difficulty of the Problems

Intuitively, the hardness of automation seems to be different for the two classes. On one hand, it seems that, at least in theory, every composition that was obtained by the instantiation of a template can also be obtained when no structure is given at all. On the other hand, the absence of limitations on control flow and data flow leaves *much* more work to do for the composition algorithm. Instead of checking a (possibly large but) finite set of variants, the set of possible compositions when no structure is given is generally infinite. This discrepance obviously induces also a difference in the complexity.

However, the range of complexities within the respective classes is quite wide, so we cannot really compare the complexity between the classes but only between approaches. For both classes, there are cases constructible that have constant time complexity and others that are undecidable. Hence, we cannot draw an overall conclusion about the hardness of the classes; the approaches must be considered individually.

The only observation we can make is that, currently, all approaches that apply to the first class decide the problem to which they are applied while there are two approaches in the second class that do not have this property. More specifically, the approaches presented in [97,109] are not guaranteed to terminate if no solution exists.

Main Conceptual A Priori Objections

The main objection against automated software composition if a structure is available is the lack of variants that must be tried. Most papers are motivated by the "enormous and evergrowing number of services", but those legions of services seem to be hidden quite effectively from potential customers in the real world. In fact, none of the approaches within this class credibly reports the (potential of an) application to an at least somewhat real world setting. Do we really have hundreds or at least dozens of operations available for each task of the template such that automation is necessary? If this is not the case, then the number of variants is relatively small, and the composition task is often trivial.

A good answer to this objection could be that variants come from *parametrization* of operations, and that, even if the set of variants is relatively small, we must give an answer in very short time, e.g., because the composition must be found at runtime of the program that embeds it. So there are actually two arguments. First, the variants may not come from many different operations but many possible parametrizations of some few ones. Second, there may be the need to find compositions on-the-fly, which, even if the set of variants is small, makes it unacceptable to configure the solutions manually.

Approaches that create compositions from scratch based on preconditions and postconditions are often faced with the objection that we cannot assume formal preconditions and postconditions to be available in real software development. This is obviously an important issue, because most papers simply assume that operations have semantic preconditions and effects given, but semantic descriptions are rare in practice. Neither do the legions of publicly available (and semantically described) services exist, nor do developers annotate functions with preconditions and effects that would make them reusable by these automation techniques.

A good answer to this objection could be that developers actually *do* provide formal specifications anyway and that specifications in form of preconditions and effects can be hardly expected unless there are powerful tools that would give a benefit to the developer. So there are also two arguments in favor of this type of automation. First, software developers do nothing else but write formal specifications all the time, namely, the implementation of functions. So specifying preconditions and effects in addition to signatures is just to specify a little more than what is specified already anyway. This becomes even more true in environments where developers are forced to provide semantic documentation such as JavaDoc. Also, the core of descriptions are rather the postconditions; preconditions may often be empty. Moreover, semantic descriptions could, at least in parts, also be derived automatically, e.g., the description of getter methods of entity classes. Second, the current non-existence of preconditions and effects is absolutely no argument that this cannot change in the future if a benefit arises for the developer. We have already seen that developers are ready to specify tons of descriptions of classes and methods where they could write a much smaller algorithm with nice goto commands. Of course, unless there is a mature composition tool that makes this benefit available to the user, no semantic descriptions can be expected.

Chapter 3
Template-Based Composition

Approaches in this class have the property that the desired composition is specified in terms of a (possibly structured) set of tasks to be carried out. That is, the structure of the desired composition is already known in advance at least on an abstract level. The remaining problem is to concretize this structure with respect to some criterion such as optimization of quality or adherence to communication restrictions of existing services.

In other words, the composition problem consists of finding a valid or even optimal *instantiation* of a given *template*. In the following, I will use the term template to refer to a structure that defines a set of tasks and a control flow and data flow definition for them using constructs such as if-statements, splits, joins, or loops. The tasks can be understood as placeholders that must be replaced by (or bound to) either concrete service operations or possibly complex subcompositions.

Since the approaches within this class are highly heterogeneous, I identify three subclasses based on the question how functional aspects drive the composition process. In this paper, I consider as functional aspects everything that has to do with what the resulting composition does in terms of the respective problem domain. For example, the task to book a flight is a functional requirement as well as the requirement that the price may not exceed a particular sum. In contrast to this, nonfunctional properties are related to properties of the composition itself, such as its price (of using the services), its execution time, trust, etc. The three subclasses are depicted in Fig. 3.1 together with their (sub)subclasses. The rough overview is as follows:

1. *Approaches that ignore functional aspects.* These approaches assume that functional issues have been resolved in advance and that an explicit set of functionally admissible service candidates is available for every task. Every placeholder is bound to exactly one service operation. The goal is to find an instantiation that possibly optimizes a goal function that aggregates the nonfunctional properties

F. Mohr, *Automated Software and Service Composition*,
SpringerBriefs in Computer Science, DOI 10.1007/978-3-319-34168-2_3

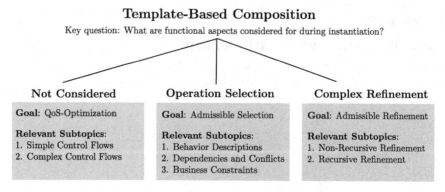

Fig. 3.1 A classification scheme for approaches that use explicit descriptions

of the chosen services along the control flow specified in the template. These
approaches are discussed in Sect. 3.1.

2. *Approaches that consider functional aspects to select concrete services.* These
   approaches bind placeholders to concrete service operations and take into account
   functional constraints such as dependencies and conflicts among operations,
   domain-specific user constraints such as traveling time etc. The goal is to identify an instantiation that satisfies the functional user requirements and possibly
   nonfunctional properties. These approaches are discussed in Sect. 3.2.
3. *Approaches that consider functional aspects to plan refinements.* These
   approaches bind placeholders to possibly complex subcompositions. In other
   words, they solve a composition problem for each of the placeholders instead of
   only binding the placeholder to a single-service operation. These approaches are
   discussed in Sect. 3.3.

It is interesting to observe that, apart from the cumulative character of the stud-
ied aspects, the approaches in the three classes form three relatively independent
research areas. Approaches in the first subclass are concerned about the question
how compositions can be optimized with respect to nonfunctional properties. This
question is also relevant for approaches in the second and third subclass, but it is
never—or at best superficially—considered. Similarly, none of the aspects considered by approaches in the second class, e.g., business constraints or transactional
properties, are considered by the approaches in the third subclass. In other words,
the approaches in the respective subclasses focus on the *augment* to the previous subclass whose major topics are largely ignored even though they are actually relevant
for them.

Note that, for better readability, the conclusion of this chapter is found in Chap. 5.
The body of the chapter is very long, and I felt that a conclusion of all approaches
is better off in the general conclusion. Of course, every section within the chapter
is closed with a conclusion in order to summarize the respective subfield; only the
general conclusion is found in Chap. 5.

3.1 Systems that Ignore Functionality

Approaches in this class assume that some explicit workflow is specified with a *finite and explicitly given* set of candidates for each task. Functional issues are assumed to have been resolved manually before, so every binding of tasks to services is functionally valid. That is, the composition algorithm receives a template with (or a set of) n tasks and candidate sets $C_1, \ldots, C_n$ where C_i is the predetermined set of candidates for task i. The set of all valid solutions is a relation $C \subseteq C_1 \times \cdots \times C_n$, which considers possible constraints on QoS values, e.g., by service level agreements. We search for an element of C that optimizes an objective function defined in terms of the nonfunctional properties. The considered nonfunctional properties are mostly the price, availability, reliability, success rate, and execution time as presented in [33].

I further divide the approaches within this subclass into those that work on simple workflows only and those that work on complex workflows. In this paper, a workflow is considered simple if its control flow is undefined, sequential, or if existing alternative branches are not treated specifically. For example, [167] considers alternative branches but simply aggregates the properties of tasks of all branches as if they were arranged in a sequence. Approaches working with simple workflows are discussed in Sect. 3.1.1. In contrast, workflows with special treatment (e.g., probabilities or maximum operator) for conditional branches and loops are considered complex. Obviously, the second model entails the first one, so every approach belonging to the second category can also solve problem instances of approaches belonging to the first one. Approaches addressing this problem are discussed in Sect. 3.1.2.

3.1.1 Simple Control Flow Models

The special property of approaches within this class is that the actual workflow of the template can be ignored. Since there are no alternative branches or loops, we know (or assume for whatever reason) that each task is executed exactly once. Hence, we simply aggregate the QoS values of the choices for the tasks.

I discuss three types of approaches. First, I introduce the basic approach proposed by Zeng et al. applying integer programming. Then, I discuss several heuristics that were proposed to improve the runtime behavior. Finally, I present three approaches that do not return a single composition but a set of Pareto optimal solutions.

3.1.1.1 Integer Programming (IP) Solution

The founding paper on automated QoS-based service composition was published by Zeng et al. [167]. The input of the composition algorithm is an activity diagram (they call it state chart) of the target composition process, where every action represents a task for which a finite set of services that implement the task is known. The output is an assignment of each task to a service that is optimal with respect to the weighted nonfunctional properties. Considered nonfunctional properties are execution price, (expected) execution duration, reputation, reliability, and availability of the services, represented as a 5-vector, each of which weighted such the total weights sum up to 1. For each quality, there is an aggregation function that allows to derive the quality of the whole composition for the respective quality. The returned solution maximizes the sum of weighted and scaled nonfunctional properties.

The composition problem is solved by linear integer programming. For each task j in the input activity diagram and each service i that may be used for task j, there is a decision variable $y_{ij} \in \{0, 1\}$ being 1 if task j is bound to service i and 0 otherwise. In addition, there are some auxiliary decision variables, e.g., for the critical paths $(z_{i,j}{}^1)$, and the aggregated values of the nonfunctional properties ($Q_{price}, \ldots$), which are expressed in terms of the basic decision variables y_{ij}. The objective function maximizes the sum over the scaled and weighted auxiliary variables for aggregated values ($Q_{price}, \ldots$).

The approach taken by Zeng et al. is an intuitive one, and, in one way or the other, each of the other approaches discussed in this section shares the underlying model. So, one can see this paper as the initial work on QoS-based service composition, and related work is mostly defined by alternative and allegedly more efficient solution methods.

In a consecutive paper, [168] extends [167] by simple loops. In a preprocessing step, these simple loops are "unfolded" into a finite sequence of conditional branches with the number being the maximum number of loop invocations observed. I am not entirely ready to accept this as an actual loop treatment, because it assumes that the composition always performs the same (maximum) number of loop iterations. A strange side-effect of this technique is also that the number of decision variables increases significantly. Computationally, this makes the model harder to solve. Conceptually, this allows the composition algorithm to select the binding for a task occurring in a loop individually for each loop run. Summarizing, the integration of loops in [168] is a nice attempt but cumbersome in the details.

3.1.1.2 Heuristic Approaches

It is intuitive to consider heuristics to relax the runtime issues associated with integer programming, but we should also have in mind that this is not necessarily the case for service composition. It is quite questionable if the instances in practice are really so huge that solving an IP is unacceptably slow or even infeasible. For example, the evaluation of several papers that propose a heuristic show that optimally instantiating a template with 20 tasks or more is done in less than five minutes, sometimes even in a few seconds. Unless this optimization is done in an on-the-fly manner—and the

---

[1]I am not fully convinced how a linear constraint can fix the value of this variable. It is a little bit curious that the paper does not describe this crucial point in more detail.

approaches in this context lack a motivation of such a setting—there is no reason to renounce optimality for runtime. So the practical relevance of the following heuristics must be judged based on the necessity to instantiate a template within fractions of a second.

Classical Heuristics

Berbner et al. were the first to develop a heuristic instantiation mechanism based on a relaxed optimization model [22]. Their algorithm (H1_RELAX_IP) works in four steps. First, the optimization problem is solved as a continuous optimization problem (LP), which can be done efficiently; this results in a solution that assigns fractions of services to tasks. Second, the candidate services for each task are ordered descendingly by the respective value of the LP solution; the algorithm will try these first. Third, the set of tasks is sorted descendingly by the number of candidates that have a value of 0 in the LP solution; the algorithm will try to fix tasks with few candidates first. Finally, they apply a backtracking algorithm that looks at each task and tries to instantiate it with candidates in the order of their sorting. If an instantiation violates the constraints, it resets the choice for the respective tasks and steps back to the previous task. The formal model seems to be sound and the evaluation shows a clear improvement of runtime compared to the integer programming case while the value of the objective function is about 99 % of the LP case.

An extremely simplifying heuristic was presented in [90]. First, the algorithm assumes that the qualities have been merged into a single utility value, one for each service and task. In addition, there is a finite number of *resources* that a service associated with a task needs. The algorithm simply chooses the services that have the best values for the resource requirements. However, the heuristic is poor not only because it does not consider the qualities separately but also because it does not even consider the merged utility in the search process. The evaluation shows that the runtime is similarly efficient than the one of H1_RELAX_IP discussed above, but the quality of solutions must be expected to be significantly worse in average. Apart from that, it is not very clear and not discussed how the parameters used in this model can be obtained in real applications.

Genetic Algorithms

Another approach based on a genetic algorithm was proposed by Xu et al. in [164]. The algorithm is an antibody-derivate of genetic programming. In each iteration, it first clones the solution candidates with the highest fitness values, then determines which service assignments occur in the majority of good candidates, and finally mutates the less-agreed service assignments. To avoid the risk of running into local optima, they use a measure called *concentration*. While the general idea of applying genetic algorithms to the problem is valid, the overall quality of the paper is rather poor. This is not only due to sloppy formalism (e.g., the fitness function is never defined) but also due to a very slim evaluation that lacks a of comparison to other approaches.

Constraint Decomposition

A heuristic approach based on constraint decomposition was presented by Alrifai et al. in [6, 7]. The idea presented in [6] is to split up every constraint, e.g., the constraint on maximum price, execution time, etc. into n new constraints for each of the n tasks of the template. The advantage is that choosing services locally optimal is much easier than choosing globally optimal due to less decision variables. Instead of choosing a local upper bound of $\frac{c}{n}$ (given the global upper bound was c), they solve a simplified IP model to compute the upper bounds of the local constraints based on a utility function, such that the sum of local upper bounds is at most the global upper bound for each quality value. While this approach is sound, it is not complete as discussed in their consecutive paper [7], because the local constraints may also cut candidates that could be contained in a global solution.

In [7], they propose two alternatives to overcome the problem of incompleteness. The paper assumes that the candidate sets only contain Pareto-optimal services; that is, services that are not dominated by others regarding the nonfunctional properties (for whatever reason, they call these services skyline services). The first returns from the local to the global optimization problem and tries to reduce the number of decision variables in the global model by reducing the candidate sets for each task using clustering. For each task, the service in the candidate set are grouped into K clusters using k-means clustering, and finally the service with the highest utility in each cluster is chosen as a representative. The second alternative pursues the local constraint approach and tries to improve the local upper bounds also based on an iterative clustering mechanism. Starting with a cluster size of one, every iteration double the number of clusters. For every cluster, a vector is defined that contains the maximum for each quality value of services within it. They then solve an optimization problem to identify the best of these bound vectors for every task. Since approach is complete, because it eventually converges to the original global problem after a sufficient number of iterations. Summarizing, the presented techniques are sound and complete, and, given the necessity of a heuristic solution, they constitute an interesting option.

Sun et al. present another such decomposition technique [146]. There is no particular novelty in comparison to Alrifai et al., only that they compute the local constraints in a different (but not obviously better) way.

3.1.1.3   A Posteriori Methods

The above approaches always produce a single solution that is hopefully on the Pareto frontier of qualities, but there are also approaches that offer the whole frontier to the user. Methods of this kind are sometimes called *a posteriori methods*. A common way to solve a posteriori optimization is through the multiobjective genetic programming algorithm NSGA-II. The difference between NSGA-II and other genetic algorithms is that it returns not only one solution but a set of (Pareto-efficient) solutions. Among the solutions returned by the algorithm, the user then can decide the preferred solution.

In spite of some attempts to solve the service composition problem using NSGA-II, the approaches in this area define a quite weak state of the art. First, Claro et al. solve the above model proposed by Zeng et al. and simply convert the constraints defining the quality variables into objective functions [40]. Unfortunately, the approach is formally flawed and the evaluation is rather poor. For example, given that the integer programming model is available, it would be the least to use it as a reference in the evaluation; however, no such comparison is made. Second, Ludwig claims to improve the former approaches by adding further user constraints in terms of service level agreements [89]. However, the paper fails to give any detailed explanation of how such constraints are actually considered in the search process. Apart from that, her approach only supports sequential workflows, which makes it quite irrelevant for practice.

An alternative solution to NSGA-II was presented by Wada et al. [158]. They work on a slightly different setting as the above approaches in that they consider service level agreements as opposed to a general objective function. The service level agreements not only define the objective function but also introduce a set of constraints for the quality values that must be achieved at least. They introduce an algorithm called E^3, which can be run with two different fitness functions; one fitness function explores for homogenous solutions while the other tries to find solutions that are very good for particular properties (and maybe significantly worse for others). The consideration and detailed description of service level agreements is an improvement of the above approaches, However, also E^3 only copes with sequential (or parallel) compositions; there is no model for alternative branches or loops. Summarizing, the approach presents a good alternative to the techniques discussed above, but the complexity of supported compositions needs to be enhanced in order to consider more realistic workflows.

3.1.2 Complex Control Flow Models

In contrast to the approaches discussed above, approaches within this class analyze the template and take the control flow into account when instantiating it. For instance, the template may contain two alternative branches one executed with probability 0.7 and one with 0.3. Then the QoS values of the operations bound to the tasks within this branch can be weighted according to these probabilities. That is, the difference to simple control flow models is that the *aggregation functions* for the properties consider the actual workflow.

3.1.2.1 Integer Programming Solution

Basic Model

Schuller et al. equip the IP model with probabilities for the different paths [134]. Probabilities are introduced for both alternative paths in conditional branches and for loops. The probability annotated for a loop is the probability that the loop body is executed once more time after its end has been reached; that is, given probability p, the probability of the loop being executed n times is p^{n-1}. Apart from this, the model is quite similar to the one presented by Canfora et al. [32]. Unfortunately, the approach is not evaluated.

Extended Model

Ardagna and Pernici apply replanning at execution time and add several other interesting aspects such as bargaining [9]. First, loops are not only unrolled assuming a maximum execution of iterations, but a probability distribution for loop cancellation is considered. The probability distribution slightly alleviates the problems induced by the unrolling technique (cf. discussion in Sect. 3.1.1 for the case of Zeng et al. [168]), but the problem of obtaining decision variables for each loop iteration remains. Second, the approach is the first in this category to consider not only services but also their operations. Tasks are assigned to both services and their operations. The advantage of this double assignment is that the model can be enhanced by restrictions that require several tasks to be bound to (different operations of) the same service. Another advantage is that nonfunctional properties can be assigned to both services and operations and be aggregated in different manners. Unfortunately, this advantage has not been exploited in the paper since all quality properties refer to operations. Third, the composition algorithm is equipped with a bargaining model that tries to negotiate over nonfunctional properties if no solution can be found for the initial query. While the idea of negotiating about these properties is nice in general, the applied model is conceptually rather disappointing. In the negotiation process, the composition algorithm (called broker) and service providers alternatively send offers and counter offers. The problem is that *both* parties *increase* their offers steadily, so instead of decreasing his requirement, the broker even increases them, reflecting a quite unnatural negotiation process. Summarizing, the paper contains significant improvements and good ideas but also exhibits some significant shortcomings to be looked at.

3.1.2.2   Heuristic Approaches

Genetic Algorithms

A genetic algorithm (GA) solution that also supports loops has been proposed by Canfora et al. [31]. The aggregation functions for nonfunctional properties distinguish between sequences, conditional branches, parallel flows, and loops. In contrast to the pessimistic estimate pursued in [168] for the runs of a loop, they use an "estimate", which probably means the expected number of runs. The fitness function of the genetic algorithm is (arbitrarily) defined as the cost plus response time divided by the availability plus the reliability plus the execution duration. The mutation of genomes simply changes the assignment of tasks to services randomly. Their evaluation shows that integer programming is better than their algorithm for small instances with at most about 20 tasks; the GA is better for bigger problems. The quality of solutions, however, is not compared between the two approaches. The main conceptual improvement compared to Zeng et al. [167, 168] discussed in Sect. 3.1.1 is the more accurate aggregation of qualities for nonsequential workflows that also takes into account the probabilities that particular branches are entered.

Canfora et al. also propose another approach that updates the composition based on the path taken at runtime [32]. Based on the offline planning method, there is an estimated quality value for the QoS values of the composition, which depends on probabilities of paths chosen at runtime and, hence, may be different for a concrete execution. For example, a priori it is estimated that a loop will be invoked k times, but at runtime we know that it has been invoked k' times, which implies that the actual QoS cause by the inner part of the loop deviates from the estimate unless $k = k'$. The same holds for paths taken in conditional control flow structures. In [32], a replanning algorithm is triggered if the deviation of the actual from the estimated QoS-properties exceeds a predefined relative threshold. In this case, the set of tasks that may be part of the remaining execution is computed; this set is called *slice*. Based on the QoS values of the already executed composition and the estimated one, the replanner tries to find a new instantiation of the slice such that the overall quality value will remain in the range of the estimated one.

The approach is rather superficially elaborated, so there are quite some issues that remain open. For example, the algorithm assumes the number of loop invocations to be known *before* its actual execution, but this number is not known until the node coming *after* the loop node is visited. Another issue is that nodes that already have been executed are also replanned, which does not make sense. The paper also lacks a comparison between no replanning and replanning, and also the rest of the evaluation is rather weak. Finally, the replanning time obviously increases the time of invocation, which is not discussed at all in the paper. Summarizing, the presented problem of replanning a workflow at runtime based on the observed execution path is interesting, but the paper leaves many questions open that are fundamental and cannot merely be considered future work.

Gao et al. present another genetic algorithm very close to the one of Canfora et al. [51]. They propose a rather complicated representation of genes based on the complete workflow, i.e., the genes include not only the services for the placeholders but also control flow nodes such as if-statements or loop heads. However, this consideration only seems to complicate the model without bringing any particular benefit. The work of Canfora is mentioned, but no real comparison is made; in particular, the evaluation does not compare the presented approach with earlier ones. One novel aspect is that the approach can also cope with soft-constraints that impose a penalty if they are violated. The fitness function is defined as the standard QoS score defined by Zeng et al. [167] minus the penalty resulting from violating the soft constraints. The overall quality of the paper is mediocre; in particular, the improvement to existing approaches is neither stressed nor proved.

Tabu Search

Ko et al. propose to use tabu search for the instantiation mechanism [73]. They consider the fact that only one of a set of conditional (sub-)paths is taken by pessimistically aggregating only the costliest one among them. The instantiation algorithm starts with a random solution and then performs a predefined number of modification steps. In each step, the algorithm randomly switches a random number of service assignments. The algorithm remembers these mutations and considers each one at most once. Depending on the improvement of the objective function and the number of the iteration, the mutation is adopted or rejected. Similar to the approach proposed by Berbner et al., their evaluation shows a clear improvement compared to the IP model. However, the quality of solutions between the heuristic and the IP model is not compared at all, so we have no information about the quality of the solutions compared to the ones found by the IP model.

Clustering

Mabrouk et al. present a clustering-based approach similar to the one presented by Alrifai et al. [92] discussed in Sect. 3.1.1. In a first step, the candidate sets for every task are clustered using K-means; the number of clusters is predefined by an expert for each task, and the clustering is performed once for each quality. Based on this clustering, they then determine the *utility* of each service for a solution. Then they introduce a threshold (called heuristic) that every service's utility must exceed to be considered. A simple backtracking algorithm then tries to find a composition that satisfied the QoS requirements. The paper quality is rather low, and there is almost no novelty compared to the approach presented by Alrifai et al. [6], which ironically appears in the references without being contained or discussed in the paper. One problem is, for instance, that average values for QoS properties are computed separately for each cluster, which means that the centroid of each cluster are computed separately for each property. But the approach later uses the membership of services to clusters (which is not unambiguous under these conditions) to compute the utility.

Relaxation

Klein et al. made two different approaches on the composition problem [68, 69, 70]. Both are based on the IP model proposed by Zeng et al.

The first approach tries to improve performance by relaxation [68, 69,]. While [68] only sketches possible solution methods, [69] uses the rounded LP solution as an initial starting point for a hill climbing algorithm. Given a parameter L, the algorithm performs $\sqrt{L}$ iterations where each iteration switches the assignment of one service and then checks if the "utility" of the solution has improved.

Despite the fact that the related work by Berbner et al. [22] is apparently unknown to Klein et al., their algorithm is neither sound nor gives it the impression to deliver good results. First, the initial solution may violate the QoS-constraints, and, even though nonviolating improvements are preferred, it is not checked if the returned solution actually satisfies the constraints. Second, the algorithm just randomly changes service assignments, which is fine using genetic algorithms, but here this is combined with a hill climbing algorithm, which can be hardly beneficial.

The second approach relies on the (faulty) assumption that the network delays in service networks cannot be considered in the other QoS-optimization approaches [70]. Therefore, they introduce delay annotations for the *edges* of the workflow. However, the network delay between the client and the service is simply the time between sending the request and receiving the answer minus the actual execution time. While it is true that the communication time depends on the position of the invoker in the network, it can simply be added to the execution time once it has been determined.

3.1.3   Concluding Discussion

We have seen that approaches within this class address a QoS-optimization problem for which either one solution or a set of Pareto-optimal alternatives is returned. In the first case, optimality is defined in terms of an objective function that somehow weights the different qualities. Whether or not this makes sense is never discussed, and, given the negative correlation between the qualities such as price and runtime, I am skeptic about the appropriateness of this assumption. In the second case, the algorithms do not return a single but a whole set of solutions, all of which are Pareto-optimal. Unfortunately, even though this model should be preferred, there are only few approaches implementing it, and they are in a rather preliminary stage. An ideal algorithm would choose the optimal solution based on a utility function that reflects the user preferences, but such an approach does not exist yet.

In the simplified case where requirements are channeled into one objective function, the problem can be solved optimally using integer programming or approximate using heuristics. The basic IP model was specified in [167] and refined with probabilities for conditional branches and loops in [134]. Heuristics are motivated by the complexity of IP and are based on relaxed LP solutions [22, 68], utilities [7, 90], or fitness functions applied to genetic algorithms [31, 164]. The first two can be considered a guided search, while genetic algorithms only rely on fitness values without the notion of a rest problem.

In spite of a considerable number of heuristic approaches, for the time being, there are no convincing arguments that they are needed. Of course, the IP approach cannot be solved efficiently for large models, but we have not seen any example of a QoS-optimization problem that could not be solved in a few seconds using advanced solvers. In fact, it is not even clear whether runtime is a critical issue. While it is easy to dream of a future where hundreds of services must be composed within fractions of seconds, we have no hint yet that such a scenario is upcoming in the soon future.

Also, the semi-multicriterial view is a frequently used but little helpful setting. Unless the client's utility function can be written as a (linear) function of the parameters whose coefficients are known in advance, this view is not appropriate. Instead, one should aim at identifying solutions on the Pareto frontier and, perhaps, try to learn the preferences by the client's choices.

Another open issue is to find a convincing treatment of loops. There is a reasonable agreement that conditional branches are either treated by probabilities reflecting the expected case or by applying the maximum operator reflecting the worst case. However, the treatment of loops is not convincing yet. In [9, 69, 168], loops are enrolled in a preprocessing using an expected number of iterations. The problem with this technique is that the semantic of the problem changes, because the duplication of the inner part of the loops implies that there are now more tasks that must be bound to services. That is, the composition algorithm now must choose a binding between tasks and services for each *iteration* of the loop; so a task occurring once in a loop is bound 10 times to possibly different services given that we expect the loop being executed 10 times. In contrast, in [32], loops are removed in a preprocessing, and the inner part of the loop is equipped with a constant k that reflects the number of actual executions and serves as a multiplicative factor for the quality values of the inner part. The problem is that this number cannot be known in advance, which is assumed in the cited paper. However, the idea is generally suited to replan the composition as soon as the loop execution has been *completed*. Finally, in [134] there is a fixed probability assigned that the loop body is re-entered, which is obviously not a good assumption. Concludingly, the support for conditional branches is satisfying whereas loops cannot be considered reasonably supported yet.

Summarizing, service composition in form of QoS-optimization has made some progress, but there are concerns regarding the relevance and some important conceptual aspects. Relatively small issues are the appropriate treatment of the multicriterial aspect and reasonable support of loops are important issues that have not been solved yet. A good approach for the first issue would be to let the instantiation algorithm be driven by a utility-function that reflect the preferences of the respective users. A reasonable loop support may model the number of iterations of a loop as a normally or exponentially distributed random variable. The most crucial objection against the approaches in the class is that the whole community depends on the claim that huge numbers of service candidates for individual tasks must be processed in fast time. However, the last decade has not brought any evidence that this scenario really exists, and no striking arguments have been reported why this should change in the future.

Table 3.1 shows the overview of the discussed approaches. The four considered features are the treatment of multicriterial aspects, whether the search is guided, and whether alternative branches or loops are considered respectively.

Table 3.1 Overview of the template-based approaches that ignore functional aspects

Name	MO	Guided	Alt	Loops	Particular Strengths	Particular Weaknesses
Zeng et al.	◐	○	○	○	first model for QoS-optimization	alternative branches treated like sequences
Berbner et al.	◐	●	○	○	LP-based heuristic, good evaluation	-
Luo et al.	○	●	○	○	-	trivial optimization model, poor evaluation
Xu et al.	○	○	○	○	strategy to avoid local optima	formally flawed, poor evaluation
Alrifai et al.	○	○	○	○	innovative heuristics, good formal description	runtime improvement questionable
Claro et al.	●	◐	○	○	a post. optimization	formally flawed, poor evaluation
Ludwig	●	◐	○	○	a post. optimization, user constraints	insufficient description of algorithm
Wada et al.	●	◐	○	○	a post. optimization, service level agreements	-
Schuller et al.	○	○	●	●	sound formal model, probabilities and loops	stochastic indepd. of probs., no evaluation
Ardagna et al.	○	◐	●	●	replanning at runtime, negotiation of QoS	negotiation conceptually flawed
Ko et al.	○	○	●	○	innovative heuristic, treatment of XOR paths	no loop support
Canfora et al.	○	◐	●	●	probabilistic model, replanning at runtime	inappropriate assumptions, rather immature
Gao et al.	●	◐	●	●	probabilistic model, soft-constraints	formally flawed, poor evaluation
Mabrouk et al.	○	◐	●	●	clustering of service candidates	novelty unclear, formally flawed
Klein et al.	○	○	●	●	considers position of client in network	conceptually weak, no novelty

MO = Multiobjective Optimization, **Guided** = Informed Search, **Alt/Loops** = Templates may contain XOR-splits/loops
● = substantially supported, ◐ = partially supported, ○ = not supported, ◉ = supported but irrelevant for automation

This table tries to summarize the discussions on the approaches of this class. The sorting within the list corresponds to the order in which the approaches were discussed. The double lines separate the approaches discussed in different subsections from each other. Literature references can be found in the respective discussions of the approaches

3.2 Systems with Functional Operation Selection

This section shows approaches that instantiate a template by binding every place-holder to a single service operation considering functional aspects. That is, for each placeholder, there is a finite set of service operations from which exactly one is chosen. Like in the previous section, the goal is to find a combination of such selections such that all constraints are satisfied and that possibly optimizes some objective function. The only difference is that functional aspects are considered in the selection mechanism.

There are several ways how functional aspects can influence the process of selecting the service operations for the placeholders of a template. First, functionality may play a role in the *discovery* of candidates for a placeholder. For example, the set of candidates for each task is not given but must be discovered in a network based on inputs, outputs, preconditions, and effects annotated to the task. Second, there could be restrictions, dependencies, and conflicts among the operations. For example, several operations may belong to one service and can only be executed in a particular order, or we may not use an operation a together with operation b in the same composition due to license issues. Functionality can also be encoded in business constraints.

The underlying model extends the model discussed in the last section by match-making and functional constraints of several types. That is, again we have n candidate sets $C_1, \ldots, C_n$ containing the admissible operations for each task. However, the set of valid solutions $C \subseteq C_1 \times \cdots \times C_n$ is defined not only by QoS constraints but also takes into account functional constraints.

The approaches are organized into three types of functional aspects that are focused. Note that these aspects are rather topics, which are not mutually exclusive. So, in theory, an approach could take into account each of the three aspects. However, most approaches in this subclass focus on one of the three topics, which is why I apply them to organize the subsection.

1. *Behavior Descriptions.* Approaches in this subclass assume that the sets $C_1, \ldots, C_n$ are not given explicitly but must first be computed as subsets from a given finite set C of available operations using a matchmaking algorithm. That is, based on some criteria such as preconditions and postconditions, the sets $C_1, \cdots, C_n$ are computed as subsets of operations of C that match the respective conditions.
2. *Dependencies and Conflicts.* Approaches in this subclass assume that the admissibility of an operation for a placeholder may be constrained by how other place-holders are bound. For example, particular operations in C_i may only be used if some specific operation c^* is chosen for C_j.
3. *Business Constraints.* Approaches in this subclass take into account global domain-specific requirement definitions of the composition. For example, the composition will create some round trip in a city and the condition is that the overall cost for the activities will not exceed 20 EUR. Typically, we have numer-ical constraints that must be satisfied by the selection of service operations.

Formally, these approaches simply complement the (nonfunctional) constraints on C by functional constraints.

3.2.1 Consideration of Behavior Descriptions

Approaches within this subclass assume behavior descriptions of placeholders on one side and operations on the other side in order to match them. The behavior is either described through inputs, outputs, preconditions, and postconditions of an operation or placeholder. This type of description is sometimes called *implicit* behavior description. Or it is described by keywords for the task that is being carried out. This type of description is sometimes called *explicit* behavior description.

3.2.1.1 Inputs, Outputs, Preconditions, and Postconditions

METEOR-S

The general idea for the METEOR-S framework is to conduct composition through replacing template placeholders with results from service discovery [3]. The basis of composition is a so called *abstract process* defined in BPEL4WS or a METEOR-S derivate of it. Unfortunately, METEOR-S uses the word template referring to *placeholders* of the abstract process, which can be confusing at first. The placeholders, which are called templates in METEOR-S, define service discovery requests. Given an abstract process and a set of constraints, METEOR-S discovers services for every placeholder such that the constraints are satisfied. Services are equipped with both functional and nonfunctional attributes, so the discovery process searches for services that satisfy the preconditions and effects defined for the respective placeholder as well as the nonfunctional properties.

While approaches in the context of the METEOR-S project are called composition approaches, the focus is more on discovery, matchmaking, and issues *around* composition. For example, in [35] the focus is on defining the similarity of ontological concepts that are used in the discovery process. Nonfunctional properties are briefly mentioned, but it is not explained how these are aggregated for the different choices. This is also true for Verma's works [153–156], which only refer to [34] for an explanation how nonfunctional properties should be aggregated. Another focus of attention is *mediation*, which deals with the problem that objects belonging to a semantic concept may have different symbolical representations, and that these may need transformation when passed among different services [156]. The most exhaustive overview over the overall instantiation approach is probably given in [139]. Also here, they call the entire process a composition process, but the only part that runs automatically in it is the discovery of services (and the execution of the composition).

Summarizing, the METEOR-S framework is centered around service composition, but automation plays a role only for isolated subproblems. The discovery, which is an important subproblem of composition, is addressed. Nonfunctional properties are considered, but rather locally; [34] does discuss the aggregation of these properties, but this is never applied in the context of the composition process. I am not aware of any dedicated automated composition algorithm in the context of the METEOR-S project.

An algorithm that would be somewhat appropriate for this context has been presented by Vallée et al. [152]. The input template is a DAG where each node is a task described by inputs, outputs, preconditions and effects, and the edges describe data dependencies between the tasks. The algorithm must bind every task to a service such that the data that are used according to the input dependencies are at least as specific as the respective types of the service used to replace the task. Context conditions are a special type of precondition that is compared with a context provided in the query. Nonfunctional properties are not considered in the approach, and no evaluation is given. Unfortunately, there is no comparison to METEOR-S.

Ontological Matchmaking

Two attempts to consider ontological types during the instantiation of templates were proposed by Lécué, Mehandjiev et al. [81, 84, 100].

First, Mehandjiev et al. propose a simple approach that replaces tasks of a given template based on functional descriptions [100]. That is, tasks and services are described through goals, inputs, outputs, preconditions, and effects. A service can be used for a task if they have the same goal, if it matches the task definition under the usual matching semantics (plug-in for types, implications for conditions). Hence, there is no conceptual innovation to much earlier approaches, say METEOR-S, except perhaps the user interface.

The second approach is very closely related to the genetic algorithms presented in the previous section [31, 164] with the difference that it considers functional aspects of tasks. Functionality is supposed to be considered through the ontological concepts associated to service inputs and outputs. In addition to two nonfunctional properties (time and price), Lécué et al. claim to also consider the matching quality of the services for the tasks.

However, there are several problems with their approach. First, one of these functional qualities relies on the number of individuals contained in the concepts of the ontology, but ontologies in service composition are often only defined in terms of concepts (only TBoxes); in fact, not even their own paper specifies an assertional box. Second, the genotypes maintained by the genetic algorithm do only consist of service selections but not of semantic links. This is only possible if there is a canonical mapping of inputs and outputs of the services to the inputs and outputs of the tasks. This mapping issue is fundamental for the approach but, surprisingly, it is not discussed at all; semantic links are not a topic at all in the discussion of the composition algorithm. Hence, the solution proposed in these papers exhibits serious conceptual flaws.

3.2.1.2   Purpose and Category

In 2003, Brahim Medjahed et al. proposed a composition approach that instantiates templates with placeholders described by categories and purposes [99]. This is somewhat similar to the abstract processes in METEOR-S, only that placeholders are functionally described not through inputs and outputs but by keywords that reflect *purpose* and *category*. Nonfunctional properties of service (operations) are fee (price), security (encrypted connection), and privacy (inputs and outputs not shown to third-party entities). A template instantiation is admissible if every placeholder is replaced by a service with an appropriate category, purpose, and if it satisfies the quality restrictions. The quality properties are not used for global optimization of the quality of the entire composition; hence, the resulting compositions are usually not optimal with respect to these qualities.

3.2.2   Dependencies and Conflicts of Operations

Approaches within this subclass assume that the choice for a service operation influences the admissibility of other operations for other placeholders. Several types of dependencies are discussed. First, the Roman model considers constraints on the invocation order of operations defined by their provider. So binding an operation to a placeholder might imply the requirement to bind a related operation to another placeholder earlier or later in the control flow of the template. Second, some approaches assume explicit dependencies or conflicts given among service operations, which may arise e.g., from license issue. Third, there are transactional approaches that try to maintain a global property of the composition (e.g., atomicity), which requires that operations are only used if they can be undone later.

3.2.2.1   Constraints on the Order of Operation Calls

Roman Model (Initial Version)

The Roman Model is an approach to automated service composition that is based on the coordination of finite state automata. It was first proposed and steadily extended by Daniela Berardi, Diego Calvanese, Giuseppe De Giacomo, Maurizio Lenzerini, and Massimo Mecella [20, 30]. In its basic version, the model consists of a finite set of services, each of which with a finite set of (parameterless) operations, which are called messages. The order in which the messages of a service can be invoked are described in a finite automaton associated with each service; the messages are the state transition labels of the automata. Similarly, a schema of the desired composition is given by a finite state automaton with transition labels corresponding to messages. The task of the composition algorithm is to bind every edge of this automaton to one of the existing services such that every sequence of messages that may be exchanged with a service is a valid path in the automaton of that service. In other words, a template in form of a finite state automaton is given with placeholders being the transitions, and the placeholders must be bound to concrete services such that their communication protocols are respected.

Even though the Roman Model is quite famous, it exhibits several quite significant conceptual shortcomings. First, when defining the template, the designer must define (i) the control flow, (ii) the *explicit names* of messages of the services that may be bound to it, and (iii) the data flow among them. But then the designer has almost done all the work already; the remaining task is only to find bindings such that the order of messages of the used services is not violated. This is only difficult if the set of messages (the so-called alphabet) is very distributed over the services, such that many services have many messages (consisting of both operation name and parameters) in common. This is rarely the case, and hence, the problem that is automated here hardly justifies the efforts demanded of the designer. Second, given that we actually have a *selection* problem of services with some constraints on the invocation order, the client is probably rather interested in nonfunctional properties (QoS). For example, he may want to have a cheapest instantiation that satisfies an expected runtime behavior. Unfortunately nonfunctional properties are not part of the Roman Model. Third, the templates may not contain loops. Taking these points into account, it is hard to imagine a practical setting where this model might find application; this suspicion is underlined by the extremely constructed examples.

Apart from this, the Roman Model does only present possible *views* on the composition problem but not a concrete technique to *solve* it. There is a sound formal problem statement given, but the part on solving the problem only ever shows how to reduce the problem to known problems, mostly the satisfiability of propositional dynamic logic (PDL) formulas. I am not aware that they have reported the actual application of a solver on either the original problem or the one to which they reduced the original problem. Even though there *may* be routines to solve those (reduced) problems, these are certainly not common knowledge, we do not know how these perform for the case of service composition. Hence, the Roman Model is a purely mathematical framework for a conceptually questionable composition problem without the ambition to actually solve it.

Colombo

There is an extension of the Roman Model called Colombo that slightly lessens the over-specification problem [19]. Colombo introduces parameters of messages and a more complex binding model. However, the parameter names are simply part of the message complete message and not parametrized by the approach; so it only seems to the human reader as if parameters are considered while this is actually not the case. The binding model between messages of the target services and the existing services in fact is slightly more advanced, but still the designer must know the exact message names. The messages specified by the designer are split up into a send message and a receive message, which mark the communication with the existing services. For example, a message *checkItem(code, avail, warehouse, price)* is split up into two messages *requestCheckItem(code, avail, warehouse, price)* and *replyCheckItem(code, avail, warehouse, price)*. So, the designer needs only to specify half of the messages and the framework automatically splits it up into two messages.

Other Related Approaches

Gerede et al. present an extension of the Roman Model that considers online composition that has some knowledge about the future at hand [52]. They point out the basic Roman model suffers from the problem that there might be not general solution for a target service but that, depending on the actual path taken within the target service for an invocation, one can partially resolve this issue. For example, the requested service shall first accept a message *a* and then a message *b* or *c*. There are two services, one accepting *a* and then *b*, and the second accepting *a* and then *c*. It is possible to bind the actions to the appropriate service but only if it is known in advance if the second message will be *b* or *c*. In [52], this is resolved with *lookaheads*, which assume that we always know the next *k* steps taken by the target service in advance. So given that in some mythical way we know what the next *k* messages will be, we know that we can exploit this information in finding a binding for the messages of the target service. While this lookahead may or may not be available in reality, the approach equally suffers from the formerly discussed problems and does not make any step towards practical relevance of the model. Note that Gerede et al. actually introduce an implementation called Wozart, which they use to *solve* the composition problem, but they do not report any evaluation.

I am only aware of two versions of the Roman Model that deal with at least some nonfunctional properties. First, Fahima Cheikh [37] introduces trust and reputation in form of credentials. A credential has a name (e.g., client status), a value (e.g., gold), and an issuer (e.g., a service or a third-party authority). The basic model is similar to the original one, but it adds *guards* to the state transitions, where guards correspond to constraints on the values of a credential or the reputation of an issuer. For example, a guard may require that a client has status *gold* and that the issuer of the credential stating that has a reputation of at least 5. These properties are, however, not part of the requirement definition (the target service) but of the available services. So it is not that the client can require that the reputation of every used service is at least 3 but that the used services have requirements on other services that shall be used together with them in one composition. This approach may make sense in environments where every service knows other services, has an opinion about them, and wants to express limitations on its usage together with other services in the same composition depending on its opinion about them. Even though this may be relevant in some settings, it does only slightly tackle the formerly discussed problems. In particular, the problem of user-based constraints on nonfunctional properties of the composition and the aggregation of such properties is not considered. Second, Mokhtar et al. [110, 111] discuss several QoS properties such as reliability, performance, cost, security, etc., but the composition algorithm is described extremely informal such that the exact process remains quite unclear; also, they do not relate themselves to the above approaches.

Only for completeness, I mention the works of Mitra et al. [102–104], but they do not seem to bring any innovation. They use a model very similar to the Colombo framework and call the services i/o automata. I cannot find any relevant novelty in comparison to the above works, and their discussion of related work suggests that the authors themselves could not either.

De Giacomo has presented a variant of the Roman model where the behavior of the target process is not described by explicit actions but by *conditions* that must be satisfied at a particular transition [44]. The task is to find a conditional composition such that for any choice of the user at runtime, a rest-composition exists that satisfies the conditions along the remaining subtree. Again, conditions are only propositional logic, but for the used setting of a smart home this seems appropriate.

One relaxation of the Roman model with respect to the message labels was presented by Huma et al. [62]. Here, the messages of the desired state automaton are not bound directly to messages with the same label of existing services, but instead message *sequences* of the desired state automaton are bound to *sequences* of messages of existing services. In particular, message sequences can be bound also if the message labels differ. For example, the message sequence *findRoom* → *viewDetails* can be bound to *getAvailableRoom*. On one hand, this allows to find more compositions and does not require that the requester knows the exact terminology (alphabet) of the community. On the other hand, this technique imposes enormous complexity issues, and it is not clear how the semantic correctness is assured. For example, it is not clear how it is made sure that the above sequence is not bound to a message *rentCar*. Hence, the approach touches an important topic, namely the relaxation of exact message name matches, but must be considered still highly preliminary.

Hassen et al. propose a variant of the Roman model where the number of service instances does not need to be bound in advance [56]. That is, in the original version, there is some a priori constant that bounds the maximum instances that may be used for each service. This constraint is removed in the above paper, and an algorithm for that "unbound" composition is given.

Markov Decision Process Model

A curious attempt to solve service composition based on finding an optimal policy for a Markov decision process (MDP) was made in [47]. The input of the composition algorithm is an MDP that is supposed to encode the possible messages that can be sent in the environment, and the output should be an optimal policy. This can be seen as a template-based approach where the MDP is the template defining the possible paths and the chosen policy is the instantiation. Unfortunately, the model is extremely flawed in several ways. First, since the returned policy should be a composition, the MDP should reflect the states of the composed algorithm. But this is not the case, because the states of the MDP correspond to the participants of the process. Second, the model lacks to define a goal state, so it is not even clear what the composition should try to achieve. The overall goal is to minimize cost, but if there is no requirement to reach a state with a particular property, then the optimal policy simply does nothing. This seems to be a general problem when applying MDP formalisms to the service composition problem. Currently, I cannot recognize that this is a fruitful path.

3.2.2.2 Dependency and Conflict Sets

A first technique that takes into account dependencies and conflicts between services was proposed by Ai et al. [4]. The approach is based on the nonfunctional model described in the previous section [167]. It adds a dependency graph and a conflict graph to the model, both of which connect concrete services that are candidates for two different placeholders. The first graph connects services s_1 and s_2 if selecting s_1 for its placeholder means that s_2 must selected as well. The second graph connects services s_1 and s_2 if selecting s_1 prohibits selecting s_2. Using the objective function as a fitness function, the composition algorithm then applies a genetic algorithm in order to find a good composition. Genes that violate the above constraints are "repaired" using a minimal-conflict hill climbing strategy. The approach claims to cope with alternative branches and loops as far as these are equipped with estimated probabilities and numbers of iterations respectively.

Liang et al. solve the same problem by combining a tabu search with a hybrid particle swarm optimization algorithm [84]. Just like in the approach taken by Ai et al., they make use of a dependency set and a conflict set for each service. Solutions that violate these constraints are stored in the (fixed) tabu set that is indexed for faster look-ups. The solutions are encoded as particles that move in an n-dimensional space where n is the number of tasks and the domain of each dimension is the number of candidates for the respective task. The evaluation suggests that the approach is better than the approach taken by Ai et al. [4] in both time and quality, but this must be relativized at least due to the fact that storing the complete tabu list in advance is notably inefficient and clearly not part of the evaluation. Summarizing, the Liang et al. present an alternative to the solution proposed by Ai et al. that may or may not exhibit better quality but that needs an on-the-fly check of constraint violation in order to be efficient.

Conflicts in terms of trust are examined by Sun [145]. Here, a trust relation is used in order to compute only compositions in which two services may only interact if their trust relation exceeds some predefined threshold, i.e., if the trust each other with at least some predefined level; this is similar to [37]. If two services do not know each other, it is tried to estimate the trust based on other trust values of similar services. It is not clear under which conditions two services are considered to interact with each other, and it is not clear why similarity of service attributes (which ones?) allows to infer assertions about trust. Also, it is not clear what conclusions can be drawn from the highly arbitrary evaluation setting. Summarizing, the idea of adding trust as an important property is reasonable, but the overall paper quality is rather thin.

3.2.2.3 Transactional Constraints

Montagut et al. proposed the consideration of transactional requirement in the context of automated service composition [112]. The input of the algorithm are a service template, a set of available services that can be used for the placeholders in the template, and a table that defines all the admissible combinations of termination states of the tasks. Termination states of a task can be *aborted, completed, failed, compensated,* and *canceled.* The algorithm then iteratively instantiates the template and filters the candidates for the currently considered task based on the former decisions. While the idea of integrating automated service composition with transactional requirements is very interesting, the paper exhibits significant formal flaws, and the algorithm description is rather superficial. Nonfunctional properties are not considered by the approach. Summarizing, the paper presents a conceptually very interesting approach that in a preliminary stage of development.

An extension of this transactional-based approach was presented by Joyce El Haddad, Maude Manouvrier, and Marta Rukoz [50]. Their approach resolves two issues of the above technique. First, in contrast to an explicit set of accepted termination states for the tasks, which can be very large, they use the notion of *risks,* which are basically profiles that subsume the termination state sets. This enables for a convenient transactional requirement definition by the user in terms of a risk profile; in their case, the user simply says whether or not she is willing to accept that the composition cannot be undone. Second, they consider nonfunctional properties. The nonfunctional properties are aggregated for the complete composition but the optimization only happens on a local level; that is, nonfunctional properties are only used to select the locally best operation for a placeholder that is admissible with respect to the transactional requirements.

The overall quality of the paper is good, but it also exhibits some shortcomings, which I discuss in some detail in order to maintain the overview.

First, the paper makes an uncommon use of the *atomicity* property, which yields two risk profiles that fail to reflect the actual user's interest. Risk 0 means that a successful execution of the achieved composition can be (theoretically) undone; e.g., for each service in it, there is another service that undos his action. But the user is probably not so much interested in a composition that can undo the first composition but that the composition itself undos its steps in case of failure of some parts of it; that is, the composition should make sure that atomicity property known from database systems by itself. Unfortunately, this capacity is ignored completely. And even if we accept their definition of atomicity, the undo-composition is not constructed, so the user does only know that he *can* but not *how to* undo the effects of the composition execution.

Second, the formal model is unnecessarily complicated in some parts. For example, they use the property *atomic* for composite web service and *pivot* for noncomposite services, but the properties have the same meaning for the approach. This distinction has a significant impact on the presentation, because they present four tables instead of one, and the automaton modeling the possible transactional states of a composition contains also more transitions. There is simply no need to treat noncomposite services in a particular way. Also, pivot and compensable (compensatable in their paper) are properties whose formal relation is not considered at all. They use p to denote the pivot property and c to denote the compensable property, but it would be much easier to simply say that a service is either compensable (p) or not compensable ($\neg p$).

Third, local QoS-optimality is not really a significant achievement, since locally optimal candidates can be computed in linear time. But I acknowledge that local optimality is better than no optimality at all.

Apart from these issues, the approach is very well described, presents a reasonable evaluation and, hence, serves as a good basis for developments in this direction, which are necessary to make it relevant for practice.

3.2.3 Consideration of Business Constraints

Business constraints express conditions in terms of the domain in which the software or service is supposed to work. In contrast to QoS, business constraints do not make assertions about the composition as a piece of software but about the solutions obtained by *applying* the composition. Typical business constraints are maximal hotel costs, traveling time, etc.

3.2.3.1 Business Constraint Satisfaction

Approaches in this section consider business constraints but do not aim at optimizing domain-specific criteria such as price of a booking etc.

Classical Constraint Satisfaction Model

Thiagarajan and Stumptner formulate the service composition problem as a constraint satisfaction problem [150]. Intuitively, the variables are the placeholders and the domains of the variables are the candidates available for the placeholder. The services are associated with attributes (e.g., price of the purchased book) that can be used by the user in order to constrain possible solutions.

The interesting aspect of the approach is that is solves the composition problem interactively with the user. In the first phase, the composition algorithm tries to find a binding of services to tasks such that the user constraints are satisfied. If no composition can be found, the user may relax the constraints once and then it is retried to find a solution. There is no further attempt, so there is at most one interaction with the user.

While adding interaction with the user is a good idea in general, I think that the degree to which it is presented in the mentioned paper is by far insufficient. The reason is that the user has no information about which constraint failed and does not know how to relax the constraints such that a solution can be found. A better solution would be to automatically compute a *set* of relaxed solutions by stripping away different sets of constraints such that possibly few constraints are removed. From this set, the user could then choose the relaxed solution that appears most appropriate to him. Hence, the approach presented in [150] is rather initial work for the respective setting.

Another problem is that it is not clear why the attribute values of the services are available at design time. For example, the price of the book determined by a service obviously depends on the book that is used as input, which is not known before execution.

Nonfunctional aspects in the sense of price of service usage, execution time, etc. are not considered by the approach.

Effect Tree Model

Küster et al. describe a composition technique based on requirement definitions in form of effect trees [78]. The input of the algorithm is a set of services and a requirement, each of which is described by a set of provided and desired effects respectively. In a way, the effects of the requests in their paper can be thought of as tasks of a template that have functional descriptions of the accepted bindings. This (imaginary) template does not have a control flow specification but there is a data flow specification among the placeholders in it, which defines a partial order between the services that will be bound to the different effects. The effect descriptions are given in form of a tree, which can also be imagined as sets of unary and binary predicates. A state then is a formula with a variable for each node in the tree and predicates corresponding to the semantics of the nodes and links between them; these predicates may connect variables with constants that represent individuals from the domain.

The composition algorithm works in two steps. First, it computes all possible bindings of services to the desired effects using a matching algorithm; every such coverage must satisfy every effect *exactly* once. In a second step, this set of candidates is filtered by removing all compositions where two services share a resource and have incompatible definitions on that resource; e.g. service 1 provides the products in a warehouse in France but service 2 cannot ship items from France. Finally, the best solution out of this set is determined and returned based on an overall matching score that can be configured by the requester.

The approach is very interesting, because it allows for complex task descriptions that also include numerical business constraints. Its major shortcomings are that no nonfunctional properties of the composition itself are considered, that compositions are only sequential, and that the formal aspects are treated very superficially; the paper is rather a sketch paper even though the techniques are verbally explained and even evaluated. For example, it is never defined what a composition is. The lack of formalism makes it somewhat difficult to build upon their technique.

3.2.3.2 Optimization Using Business Constraints

Channa et al. present an integer programming optimization model similar to the one proposed by Zeng et al. but considers business constraints [36]. The approach assumes a template with placeholders given, and for each placeholder the finite set of candidates is known. The user constraints are encoded into an LP program that tries to minimize business goals, e.g., the price of a transaction considering also other business domain constraints such as supply time. While the overall idea of the approach is innovative, its technical elaboration is largely insufficient. First, the formal model is heavily flawed (templates are never formally introduced), and inner parts of the constraints are defined as sets instead of vectors. Second, the QoS properties are mentioned but not really considered in the model. Third, multicriterial aspects are completely ignored. Apart from that, no discussion of relevant related work such as Zeng et al. is given.

Hassine et al. present an approach that considers user preferences on business constraints of solutions [57]. Constraints can be either soft or hard. Hard constraints must be satisfied, and soft constraints *may* be satisfied and induce a *penalty* in the case they are not. In addition, for every service i and every placeholder j, a constant value denotes the user's *preference* that i is used for j; the preferences for a placeholder do not necessarily add up to one, so the term *utility* would be more appropriate. The algorithm tries to find the solution that has the best net utility, that is, the highest sum of preferences minus the penalties for violated soft constraints. The type of constraints introduced in this paper is quite interesting, but there are also some flaws. For example, the approach does not contain any evaluation, and the formalism contains several errors. Another problem is that the approach requires that the user has an explicit opinion about every service, which is not the case in practice.

3.2.3.3 Rule-Based Domain Constraints

Karakoc and Senkul present a template-based approach quite similar to the METEOR-S framework (cf. Sect. 3.2.1.1) [66, 67]. The composition template is given in advance with the tasks being specified semantically. However, the papers leave the concrete description language quite vague, and no discovery mechanism or matchmaking interface is described; one may assume that the descriptions are supposed to be similar to what is used in METEOR-S. The novelty is that conditional constraints on both QoS values and service selection. For example, "If both Ski and Balloon activities exist in holiday program, then total cost can cost $100 more" [67]. Constraints on the instantiations are of the form "If Web service template WT1 is done by Web service W1, then Web service template WT2 must be done by the same/different Web service", where "web service template" means what we understand by a placeholder. In general, the problem is not very exciting, because solving this kind of problem is rather trivial. This is also reflected in the evaluation, which shows that, even for this nonoptimized approach, the instantiation even for large templates (60 control flow nodes) and many candidate service (over 1000) can be done within less than a second. Curiously, Karakoc and Senkul claim in the introduction of [67] to consider quality of service (QoS) properties, which they effectively do not in either of the papers. Also, they are apparently not aware of the approach by Hassine et al. [57] and Thiagrajan and Stumptner [150].

A slightly different but also rule-based composition algorithm was proposed by Zeng [169]. The input of the composition algorithm is a raw version of the desired composite service and a set of so called forward dependencies and backward dependencies. The composite service is described by an activity diagram and must be refined using the dependencies, each of which is bound to exactly one activity.

Forward dependencies say which other activities (tasks) must be executed after the activity it refers to, and backward dependencies say which other activities must be executed before it. The challenge in this setting is that the conditions partially depend on values that become available at runtime only. First, the backward dependencies are applied. Then, the resulting composition is executed and, if necessary, the composition is extend online using the forward dependencies. It is hard to judge this approach, because it is kept relatively vague and the examples sometimes have little to do with software services. However, my overall impression is that it has nothing to offer that cannot also be done with HTN planning (even though they claim the opposite).

3.2.4   Concluding Discussion

What we have seen in this section is that there is a wide range of approaches that pick some specific functional aspect and create a composition algorithm that is tailored for it. The main aspects are (i) discovery and matchmaking for the candidates of the placeholders, (ii) dependencies and conflicts among operations, and (iii) business constraints. There is no general incompatibility among these features, so there is no reason why there could not be a composition framework that considers all of these aspects (and even nonfunctional properties) at the same time at least in theory.

Besides the particular strengths and weaknesses of the approaches, Table 3.2 considers six criteria that may be considered. First, the consideration of nonfunctional aspects as described in the previous section, which is fully supported if they are globally optimized and partially if they are considered at all. The criteria abbreviated by *Mat*, *Dep*, and *Bus* refer to the consideration of matchmaking between placeholders and operations, dependencies and conflicts among operation selections, and business constraints respectively. These columns show that there are only few approaches that consider several of these aspects at a time, which is why the above organization of subsections is almost a partition with respect to these criteria. Next, there is a criterion that says whether or not an approach interleaves the composition process and the execution process. This is a particularly important criterion for business constraint approaches, because choices may depend on concrete results obtained at execution time. However almost none of the examined approaches takes interleaving into account. Finally, since loops are a particular challenge for the composition task, there is a criterion that says whether or not the approach can work with loops.

The approaches that focus on discovery and matchmaking become composition approaches basically by considering some global aspect such as nonfunctional properties of the composition. If only the matchmaking problem is considered as, e.g., in [100, 152], then the term composition only refers to a fixed number of matchmaker invocations; the relation to a composition task is rather thin.

Table 3.2 Overview of the template-based approaches that use functional aspects to *select* service operations for placeholders

Name	QoS	Mat	Dep	Bus	Int	Loops	Particular Strengths	Particular Weaknesses
METEOR-S	●	●	○	●	○	○	may aspects considered	only description but no formal algorithm
Mehandjiev et al.	○	●	○	○	○	○	user interface implemented	no conceptual novelty
Lécué et al.	◑	●	○	○	○	○	ontological semantics	conceptually flawed
Vallée et al.	○	●	○	○	○	○	considers context information	no formal algorithm, no QoS, no evaluation
Medjahed et al.	◑	●	○	○	○	◑	explicit placeholder descriptions	simplistic functional view
Berardi et al.	○	○	●	○	○	○	good formal model	simplistic functional view, no algorithm
Gerede et al.	○	○	●	○	◑	○	good formal model	simplistic functional view, lookaheads unrealistic
Cheikh et al.	◑	○	●	○	○	○	considers trust as one QoS	simplistic functional view, no algorithm
Mokhtar et al.	●	○	◑	○	○	○	considers several QoS	no formal model, algorithm description superficial
Mitra et al.	●	○	●	○	○	○	considers cost as one QoS	simplistic functional view, only one QoS
De Giacomo et al.	○	○	◑	○	○	○	relaxes exact matches	simplistic functional view
Huma et al.	○	◑	●	○	○	○	relaxes exact matches	soundness unclear, preliminary stage
Hassen et al.	○	○	●	○	○	○	relaxes bound on instances	simplistic functional view
Doshi et al.	○	○	●	○	○	○	-	formally and conceptually flawed
Ai et al.	●	○	●	○	○	●	-	functional aspect is very small
Liang et al.	●	○	●	○	○	●	-	functional aspect is very small, unfair evaluation
Sun	◑	◑	●	○	○	●	consideration of trust	formally weak
Montagut et al.	○	○	●	○	○	○	transactional aspects	formally weak
El Haddad et al.	●	○	●	○	○	○	transactional aspects	QoS locally only, compositions not atomic
Thiagarajan et al.	○	○	○	●	○	○	user interaction	poor implementation of interaction
Küster et al.	○	○	○	●	○	○	user preferences	superficial formalism, only sequences
Channa et al.	◑	○	○	●	○	○	-	formally flawed, no evaluation
Hassine et al.	○	○	○	●	○	○	user preferences	formally flawed, no evaluation
Karakoc et al.	○	●	○	●	○	◑	conditional constraints	descriptional aspects unclear, formally flawed
Zeng et al.	◑	○	●	●	○	○	self-adaption of compositions	rather business process than software composition

QoS = Quality of Service (NF-Properties), **Mat** = Matchmaking for Behavior Descriptions of Placeholders, **Dep** = Dependencies and/or Conflicts Among Operations, **Bus** = Business Constraints, **Int** = Interleaving Composition and Execution, **Loops** = Loop Treatment
● = substantially supported, ◑ = partially supported, ○ = not supported, ◕ = supported but irrelevant for automation

This table tries to summarize the discussions on the approaches of this class. The sorting within the list corresponds to the order in which the approaches were discussed. The double lines separate the approaches discussed in different subsections from each other. Literature references can be found in the respective discussions of the approaches

The Roman model offers an elaborate formal basis but does not present any concrete algorithm, and, without improved consideration of QoS, its utility is highly questionable. It would be certainly beneficial to see evidence for the practical applications of the model and that the automation compensates the efforts necessary to formalize services and the query. I think that the use case for the Roman model is the same than the one for the QoS-optimizing tools discussed in the previous section where constraints on the invocation order shall be considered like in [9]. Unfortunately, the consideration of QoS in the scope of the Roman model [37, 104] stands back even behind the simplest techniques of the QoS-community, so a lot of work has to be done to make the model suitable for its actual use case. The good news is that the functional aspects considered in the Roman model would be a great complement for the efforts in QoS-optimization, so this combination would certainly be a step into the right direction.

The approaches related to business constraints introduce an interesting conceptual aspects but are technically disappointing. The business constraints presented in [57, 67, 150, 169] are certainly interesting and could also be included into the other paradigms. However, the context in which they are presented is very isolated from existing standards and tools on service composition and little convincing.

Similarly, the remaining approaches bring some interesting isolated aspects with them but do hardly constitute a relevant composition solution themselves. For example, the transactional approaches [50, 112] or the usage of purposes to tag operations [99] are individually interesting aspects. However, the considered aspects by themselves are probably not strong enough to constitute a relevant composition problem, so they must be combined with other existing aspects. A first step into this direction was already done by El Haddad et al. through the consideration of QoS, but the lack of a sufficient consideration of functional aspects is still a major concern.

3.3 Systems with Placeholder Refinement

Approaches within this section instantiate a template by refining every placeholder to a possibly complex subcomposition. That is, the set of candidates for the placeholders is not a set of atomic service operations but of possibly complex structures that are not explicitly predefined. The goal of composition is to find a combination of such subcompositions such that all constraints are satisfied and that possibly optimizes some objective function.

We can distinguish recursive from nonrecursive refinement approaches. Nonrecursive refinement approaches assume that there are no potential structures predefined for the subcompositions that may be used to refine the placeholders. Recursive approaches assume that the candidates that can be used to refine a placeholder are either atomic service operations or templates themselves.

3.3.1 Nonrecursive Refinements

3.3.1.1 Golog-Adpation

The first template oriented composition approach I am aware of is McIlraith's and Son's one adapting the Golog language [98]. They use the term *action* to refer to service operations. Templates are formulated in the form of Golog programs, which may contain sequences, tests, nondeterministic choices of actions and arguments, and loops.

The important difference to common programs is that the control flow contains nondeterminism in the sense that the program may "choose" at runtime how to proceed. That is, during the execution of a Golog program δ, the executing interpreter may hit a statement of the form $\delta_1 | \ldots | \delta_n$. This statement means that it shall proceed with one of the programs $\delta_1, \ldots, \delta_n$, but it is up to the interpreter to choose which one.

Automated composition comes into play when trying to find a possible execution run of a given program. The composition algorithm has two inputs, the Golog program (the template) and the user constraints, which may define a certain budget or logical constraints. The template is defined once for many use cases, and the constraints define a subset of possible execution runs of the template. In other words, the nondeterministic choice points of the generic program δ implicitly induce a set of possible execution runs, and the task is to identify one execution run that is compatible with the user constraints.

In order to determine the satisfaction of user constraints, the composition algorithm interleaves planning and execution. The composition algorithm applies a read-only interpreter to perform the candidate execution runs; read-only means that it executes only operations that gather information while it *simulates* the invocation of world-altering operations (assuming default behavior). If an execution run that is compatible with the user constraints is found, it is returned as a solution.

The approach is semi-recursive, because placeholders can be replaced by complex constructs but replacements of this type cannot be done arbitrarily often. That is, on one hand, the nondeterministic choice points, which are placeholders of the template, may cause the interpreter not only to consider a single action but whole subprograms. This implies that the interpreter replaces the structure with a program that may contain placeholders itself. On the other hand, the complete (nondeterministic) program is specified in advance, so the depth up to which this kind of recursion can happen is bound by the template.

While the approach is conceptually interesting, it has not been sufficiently elaborated and evaluated to be considered mature. There are some good motivating examples that show the general feasibility, which is not surprising. However, the approach has never been evaluated. Technically, the approach has only been implemented on the basis of Prolog, which requires an explicit database given; this is usually not the case in a service environment. Another problem is the way how formalism is used to describe the approach. On one hand, the paper is very formal and introduces some extremely detailed aspects such as the IRP assumption. Some aspects are not even necessary for the paper, such as the so-called *order construct*, which can be used to apply recovery routines online. On the other hand, it misses to point out very fundamental elements. For example, the paper does not give a formal statement of the addressed problem. Finally, nonfunctional properties of the composition such as runtime and price of components is completely ignored. Consequently, the approach corresponds to an interesting idea, but its description is too vague and due to its low evaluation, it cannot be considered mature; the lack of consecutive research seems to affirm this observation.

3.3.1.2 Alternative Templates

Oster et al. take an approach that considers several potential solution structures for a query [116, 117]. Functional requirements are described as a propositional logical formula Θ represented in form of an AND-OR-tree, where the leafs correspond to requirement keywords. The formula Θ asserts which functionalities may be satisfied together in order to satisfy the query but there is no notion of a control flow or a data flow. Intuitively, every conjunction of this formula in disjunction normal form can be seen as a specification of a template with where each literal is a task. Nonfunctional properties are quantitative or ordinal in [117] and set-based in [116]. In [117], for every leaf node in Θ, there is a set of services satisfying the respective functional requirement, each service having a price, a throughput, and a reliability. Starting with the leafs of Θ, they use a bottom-up propagation of nonfunctional properties to identify the selections of services that are not dominated by others; hence, a set of Pareto optimal solutions is computed.

The approach in [116] differs in two ways from most other techniques discussed in this survey. First, the leafs of Θ are already bound to concrete services; hence Θ actually does not define a template but a set of solutions already. Second, nonfunctional properties are expressed not in values of categories but as propositions. To this end, they create a set of *profiles* of nonfunctional properties, which are simply sets of propositions. The set of profiles is ordered by the user preferences using a technique called Conditional Importance Networks (CI-nets). Every service has a set of properties it supports and a set of properties it eliminates if contained in a selection. Starting with the "best" profile, they try to find a selection that is satisfies the functional requirements on one hand and the respective profile on the other hand. In both papers, the result of the process is a *set* of services without control flow and data flow. [116] mentions a phase of composing and verifying the selected services, but the utility of this approach is quite questionable given that the only requirement definition for that composition is that "services $s_1, \ldots, s_n$ must be used in it".

A similar approach was taken by Barakat et al. where the template is not described by a single workflow but by a *set* of possible workflows [13]. A task is simply a label, and the possible decompositions of a task are described in a graph structure; this structure induces a set of possible abstract workflows, which are sequential.

The novelty of the approach is then that the algorithm does not only search for the best local selection but for the best decomposition of the overall task.

3.3.1.3 Simple Planning

Kalasapur et al. try to replace a task of the user query with an on-the-fly created sequence of services if no existing one can be used to instantiate it [65]. Tasks are functionally described in terms of input and output types, and services are described by state charts with transitions corresponding to data that flows between the (sub)services; input and output transitions of the whole diagram mark inputs and outputs of the service. The input for the composition algorithm is a set of tasks and a set of service descriptions. The goal is to bind every task to a service composition. The algorithm first tries to bind a task to a single service if such a service can be matched based on the inputs and outputs. If no such service exists, they try to find a chain of services that starts with the task inputs and can produce data of the types of the task outputs. To achieve this, they apply a shortest path search in a so-called parameter graph, which consists of data nodes and arcs corresponding to services indicating how particular data types can be achieved. The second step is very close to what Hashemian et al. do in [54, 55], which I discuss in Sect. 4.1.2, and the problems are quite similar. For example, it is not clear whether the all the inputs of the services found for the composition are provided at all. For this reason, and due to the fact that the approach lacks a concise formal description, it fails to convince for the property of soundness.

3.3.1.4 Composition Through Interpretation of Unknowns

Srivastava et al. describe an approach to software synthesis that is based on theorem proving for FOL formulas with *unknowns* [143]. Unknowns can be understood as existentially quantified literals that must be bound to concrete formulas by the theorem prover; hence, the problem is actually a *second*-order logic satisfiability problem. The composition problem is described by a so called scaffold that contains (i) preconditions and postconditions as FOL formulas, (ii) the available operations and expressions usable for conditions, (iii) an abstract control flow template, and (iv) restrictions on temporary variables and operation calls that the composition must adhere to. The template only defines the general control flow structure, for instance acyclic code followed by a loop with arbitrary acyclic body. For a fixed parameter n, the template is *expanded* into an abstract control flow that introduces one loop head for each loop occurring in the template and n if-then-statements for each acyclic block occurring in the template. For each condition (of loops and if-statements) and for each statement, an unknown is introduced for the guard, and for each loop, an unknown is introduced for the invariant. The algorithm then derives a second-order logic formula called the *synthesis condition* that encodes the conditions that must be true in order for any template instantiation to be correct. In the next step, a second-order SMT (SAT modulo theories) solver is used to bind the unknowns to concrete (problem specific) formulas and to check whether the respective binding satisfies the required behavior.

Similar to the case of term algebraic synthesis discussed in Sect. 4.3.3.1, the main difference to classical service composition is that operations are described by their implementation. For instance, the postcondition of a service operation may be a predicate $AvailabilityOf(y, x)$ where y is the availability of an item x. There is no information of how this predicate is computed; the implementation is *hidden* in the operation. In contrast, operations in the approach by Srivastava et al. are described by their implementation. For example, an operation $y = 2 \cdot x + 4$ says that the output of the operation, which is y will be $2 \cdot x + 4$, so x is an input of the operation. Not only the designer but also the composition algorithm know the semantics of that implementation, so the composition algorithm can exploit the knowledge about the implementation of operations. In particular, knowing the space from which operations stem, the composition algorithm can create arbitrary new operations on the fly, e.g., $y = 3 \cdot x^2 + k$, depending on the underlying theory.

It is not trivially clear how this type of program synthesis relates to automated service composition. On one hand, the approach benefits from the built-in theories available for the composition algorithm, because this allows for the encoding of many different problems on the basis of a rather small vocabulary. That is, only using the theories of linear algebra, we can already encode several problems that can be addressed with the approach, e.g. swapping two variables without using temporary variables, matrix multiplication, or integral square root computation. On the other hand, the tight coupling between implementation and description of operations, which are bound to very narrow domains such as integers make the approach little flexible. In fact, all of the presented examples work on the numerical domain, and the operators do not have preconditions except that the inputs are numbers. The framework would require a quite significant adaption to support operations that have more complex preconditions than only types. Another problem is the tremendous complexity, because the number of operations is usually infinite, so searching for good instantiations of the unknowns is a quite challenging task. But complexity is also an issue of other service composition approaches, so this is not a particular drawback of their technique.

3.3.2 Recursive Refinement

This section treats approaches that assume that placeholders are replaced by instances of other subtemplates. That is, for each placeholder, there is a set of candidate templates, and each of them can be instantiated again (in the same way) in order to obtain an instantiation of the top-level template.

3.3.2.1 HTN Planning

Hierarchical Task Networks (HTN) are a powerful AI planning concept that allow to create plans by recursive refinement of *tasks*. A task is nothing more than the *name* representing some activity. For some tasks, there is an operation that implements them; these tasks are called *primitive*. Tasks for which such an implementation does not exist are *complex* and must be refined before they can be executed. A task network is a partially ordered set of tasks. Given an initial task network, HTN planning tries to refine the network to a sequence of actions (ground operations). Since some of the tasks may be complex, these cannot be replaced directly by actions but must be broken down first. This is done through so-called *methods*, which define how a complex task can be substituted by another task network.

Initial Approach

HTN Planning was first applied to service composition by Dan Wu, Bijan Parsia, Evren Sirin, James Hendler, and Dana Nau [163]. The obvious analogy to services is that primitive tasks are atomic processes while complex tasks are simple or compound processes in the sense of DAML-S/OWL-S. Simple processes are simply abstract one-step processes that are refined by an atomic or a complex process. Hence, simple processes define a task network with only one task with one method for each atomic or composed service that can be used to refine it. Compound processes define a control flow that may contain other processes, which can be directly translated into a task network with the tasks corresponding to the processes contained in the compound process. Given the control flow of a desired compound process, they use HTN planning to successively ground the tasks to actions. Atomic processes in the desired process are directly bound to the respective service, while simple and compound processes are recursively refined.

The service composition problem that is addressed here is extremely close to the one by McIlraith et al. In a more detailed version of the approach, Sirin define the semantics of the OWL-S based composition on the action theory approach proposed by McIlrraith et al. [138]. Atomic processes correspond to actions and compound processes to programs in [98]. Simple processes correspond to the nondeterministic choice points. A major difference, which Sirin et al. fail to point out, is that Golog programs cannot call subroutines, which avoids endless recursion. In other words, the OWL-S process model used for HTN-based planning is more expressive than the Golog variant proposed in [98]. This also enables a modularized representation of the desired process.

The initial HTN-based approach exhibits some conceptual improvement of the Golog approach, but the main critics remain. First, also the evaluation of HTN-based service composition is very thin. While the initial works [138, 163] do not contain any evaluation at all, at least a preliminary evaluation is given in [137]. Second, I think that the approach in the presented form misses the actual point of interest. The challenging and interesting aspect of this type of service composition is neither translation from OWL-S processes to HTN methods and operations (which is straight forward) nor the optimization of composition runtime. The fast runtime shown in the evaluation underlines the intuition that runtime is not an issue in a pure process refinement setting. Instead, the consideration of both functional and nonfunctional constraints would be of much more interest; out of all the possible refinements, which is the best according to the nonfunctional properties considering a certain budget or the user preferences? However, these questions are not tackled at all, which is even worse given their claim to show how to "encode both hard constraints about the functional parameters of the services and soft constraints related to nonfunctional attributes of the services" [138], which is simply not true.

Extented Approaches

In the next step, Sohrabi et al. [140, 141], Lin et al. [87] independently added constraints in order to model functional user preferences. The constraints are similar to classical HTN constraints and say which logical conditions should be true at which point in the task network. In order to adopt the composition goal to the user constraints, Sohrabi et al. introduce preference formulas that order the importance of constraints, and Lin et al. introduce a violation function that punishes the violation of constraints by a constant factor. For example, they allow for statements like "Lara prefers direct economy flights with a Star Alliance carrier, followed by economy flights with a Star Alliance carrier, followed by direct economy flights with Delta airlines" [141]. This is a nice extension, because it allows to guide the template instantiation process by this kind of user preferences. Nonfunctional properties of the services are still not considered.

The consideration of nonfunctional properties, at least in a rudimentary form, was brought to HTN-based service composition by Chen et al. [38]. In [38], the basic HTN algorithm is extended to cope with availability, reliability, cost, and response time of services, which are merged in a reward function R. Every decomposition with a reward value R smaller than some previously set threshold λ is rejected. Nonfunctional properties can be computed only for sequential processes and are considered with a particular weight. They argue that HTN-plans are sequences of operators and that, hence, the nonfunctional properties can be simply merged for sequences of operations. But this is a mistake, because the primitive tasks could also indicate the beginning or the end of a loop; hence, the composition is a sequence of control flow elements, but the *semantics* of the elements could indicate alternative branches or loops.

Another question addressed for this type of composition was how to proceed in the presence of several sources of semantics [86]. The paper tackles the question how the knowledge of several ontologies can be merged in order to obtain the desired results in the composition process. However, user constraints or nonfunctional properties do play no role in that approach.

This said, there have been some efforts on service composition through HTN planning, but no mature approach considering more than only one interesting aspect at a time has been presented yet. In its infancy, constraints were claimed to be relevant, which is true, but they were de facto ignored. Later, user constraints and nonfunctional properties were considered, but only in a rudimentary fashion and independently from each other. An integrated approach of HTN-based service composition has not been presented. While this type of service composition would be very interesting in practice, the presented approaches failed to advance the technology to a sufficiently mature (and usable) degree.

As a final remark, we should keep in mind that HTN is a general planning technique that can do *much* more than what has been done so far in HTN-based service composition. In fact, this paper presents HTN-based service composition as a template-instantiation mechanism, but the fact that HTN planning can also encode classical planning tasks shows us that we can use the HTN calculus for much more than it has been used up to now. Even though this is its most intuitive application, it would be wrong to associate HTN planning only with recursive template instantiation.

3.3.2.2 Composition Through Abduction

Aydın et al. present an approach that applies abductive theorem proving in the event calculus in order to solve the composition problem [12]. The approach is closely related to the GoLog and HTN planning approaches. The input of the algorithm is a generic workflow encoded in terms of event axioms, the user inputs and business constraints, e.g., maximum driving time, and the goal state, e.g., that a trip from Ankara to Athens has been planned for a particular date. Abduction is a logical calculus in which for a background theory T and a set of literals O (the observations), a set of literals E that are an explanation for the observation is search. Formally, the task is to find a set of literals E such that $E \wedge T$ is satisfiable and $T \wedge E \models O$. In service composition, the set T consists of the service descriptions, O of the desired goal state, and E is a set of actual invocations of the existing services.

The comparison to HTN planning for service composition is straight forward. The desired composition is described by the name of the problem to be solve, e.g., $travel(O, D, D_1, D_2)$; this is what would be a simple process in OWL-S and a complex task in HTN planning. Axiom correspond to methods in that they describe how a task can be decomposed. The conclusion of the axiom defines the task that is accomplished by the subprocess, and the premise defines the decomposition; hence, this is only a syntactic difference. Aydın et al. claim that their approach is more powerful than the HTN-based technique because it allows for services with that are information gathering and world-altering at a time, while HTN-based composition would be restricted to services that are exclusively one of the two types. However, this is not a striking argument, because the difference of outputs and effects in OWL-S is rather artificial and not very relevant for composition.

The main contribution of Aydın et al. is not so much to solve a new class of problems but to bring a new paradigm to service composition. In fact, abduction is a very natural way to see the service composition problem, and this observation is even independent from the fact whether the desired composition is described explicitly or implicitly. In fact, in Sect. 4.1.2, I discuss an approach building on top of this work but being based on input and output descriptions [115]. The great advantage of standard logical approaches is that we can use existing tools, i.e., theorem provers, to solve the composition problem. With respect to nonfunctional properties, they briefly claim to construct the plans based on quality of services, but the description on this part of the composition is so slim that we cannot consider it a serious treatment of the issue. Summarizing, the paper is an initial work whose major contribution is to bring together logical abduction and a variant of the automated service composition problem, for which other solutions already existed.

3.3.3   Concluding Discussion

Like in the previous section, Table 3.3 considers six criteria that may be considered by approaches within this subclass. First, the consideration of nonfunctional aspects as described in the previous section, which is fully supported if they are globally optimized and partially if they are considered at all. The criteria abbreviated by *Mat*, *Dep*, and *Bus* refer to the consideration of matchmaking between placeholders and operations, dependencies and conflicts among operation selections, and business constraints, respectively. These columns show that there are only few approaches that consider several of these aspects at a time, which is why the above organization of subsections is almost a partition with respect to these criteria. Next, there is a criterion that says whether or not an approach interleaves the composition process and the execution process. This is a particularly important criterion for business constraint approaches, because choices may depend on concrete results obtained at execution time. However almost none of the examined approaches takes interleaving into account. Finally, since loops are a particular challenge for the composition task, there is a criterion that says whether or not the approach can work with loops.

The approaches based on HTN planning suffer from a similar problem as the Roman model. On one hand, they are formally well elaborated and introduce quantitative business requirements such as traveling time, budgets, etc. On the other hand, we have not seen an exhaustive example that would clearly demonstrate the necessity of applying the technique. Also here, the convincing use case seems to be rather in the QoS-optimization of the (recursive) template instantiations. It has not become clear that there actually is a need for this recursive type of template instantiation, but in case it was, quality of service would be an important issue. The efforts on including QoS into HTN-based service composition made in [38] are only a first step into that direction.

Table 3.3 Overview of the template-based approaches that use functional aspects to *refine* placeholders by subcompositions

Name	QoS	Mat	Dep	Bus	Int	Loops	Particular Strengths	Particular Weaknesses
Kalasapur et al.	○	●	○	○	○	○	different degrees of locality of services	no formal algorithm, probably unsound
Oster et al.	●	○	○	○	○	○	keywords as functional requirements	simplistic functional view, formally flawed
Barakat et al.	●	○	○	○	○	○	hierarchical task specification	weak formal model, evaluation & comparison
Srivastava et al.	○	●	○	○	○	●	complex compositions, precd., and eff.	implementation=description, complexity
McIlraith et al.	○	○	○	●	●	◉	practical applicability demonstrated	formal model not concise
Wu, Sirin et al.	○	●	○	○	●	◉	formally sound, real recursion	poor evaluation
Sohrabi et al.	○	●	○	●	●	◉	formally sound, considers preferences	-
Lin et al.	○	●	○	○	●	◉	formally sound, considers preferences	-
Chen et al.	●	●	○	○	●	◉	only HTN model with QoS	formally flawed, no preferences
Aydin et al.	○	●	○	●	●	◉	abduction logic	no preferences, no evaluation

QoS = Quality of Service (NF-Properties), **Mat** = Matchmaking for Behavior Descriptions of Placeholders, **Dep** = Dependencies and/or Conflicts Among Operations, **Bus** = Business Constraints, **Int** = Interleaving Composition and Execution, **Loops** = Loop Treatment
● = substantially supported, ◑ = partially supported, ○ = not supported, ◉ = supported but irrelevant for automation

This table tries to summarize the discussions on the approaches discussed in this class. The sorting within the list corresponds to the order in which the approaches were discussed. The double lines separate the approaches discussed in different subsections from each other. Literature references can be found in the respective discussions of the approaches

Chapter 4
Composition Without a Given Structure

Every approach discussed in this section solves some form of a planning problem. A planning problem asks for a sequence of actions that an agent must perform in a problem domain Σ in order to reach a goal situation s^* starting from an initial situation s_0. The problem domain Σ is defined based on a logical language $\mathcal{L}$, which may be propositional logic or (some variant) of first-order logic. It consists of a countable set of states, a countable set of actions that can be performed by the agent, and a state transition function that defines how the agent can move through the state space through actions. The states are described as formulas over $\mathcal{L}$, and the initial state s_0 and goal state s^* belong to the state space.

The analogy between AI planning and automated service composition is as follows. Let us assume that we want to find the *implementation* for a service operation for which we currently have only a signature and logical preconditions and postconditions. The preconditions describe knowledge that may be assumed to be true at time of invocation, and the postconditions say what is true after the (successful) invocation. Then, we can think of this as a planning problem where the initial situation s_0 corresponds to the preconditions, the goal situation s^* to the postcondition, the state space corresponds to the semantic states of the thread that will later execute the implementation, and the actions correspond to invocations of existing service operations.

The service composition problem addressed this way is not generally a *classical* planning problem [105]. Classical planning, which is subject of almost all available planning tools, assumes that the state space of the planning domain is finite. This is often possible even if $\mathcal{L}$ is a first-order logic language by *grounding* the predicates using a finite set of objects that is assumed to exist in the environment. However, in the case of software composition, this set of objects corresponds to the data containers (programming variables) that are used to pass data between operations, and the number of these containers is not bound in general.

© The Author(s) 2016

F. Mohr, *Automated Software and Service Composition*,
SpringerBriefs in Computer Science, DOI 10.1007/978-3-319-34168-2_4

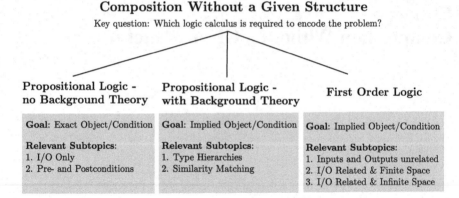

Fig. 4.1 Composition problems where no structure is given

We can identify three subclasses for the approaches within this class based on the underlying logical language $\mathcal{L}$. Figure 4.1 shows an overview over the three subclasses.

1. Many approaches *canonically correspond* to a propositional logical planning problem in that there is exactly one planning action for each service operation with an obvious translation. Section 4.1 discusses these approaches.
2. Many approaches use some sort of (possibly first-order) background knowledge such as type hierarchies that must be encoded in additional planning actions. The transformation to a classical planning problem can be done in linear time. These approaches will be discussed in Sect. 4.2.
3. The third subclass comprises approaches that are based on FOL, which are discussed in Sect. 4.3. Here, operation descriptions may contain predicates with two places or more. Not all of these encodings can be reduced to propositional logic, and if they can, this translation cannot be done in polynomial time.

The main difference between the first two subclasses and the third one is that only approaches in the third subclass allow to relate data to each other and to model the data flow. Approaches discussed in Sects. 4.1 and 4.2 assume that we have only unparametrized knowledge about data; e.g., that an object x *is* a client but not that he is *attended* by some employee y unless y is fixed a priori. Hence, approaches in the third subclass are an order of magnitude more expressive than the approaches in the first two subclasses.

Note that, for better readability, the conclusion of this chapter is found in Chap. 5. The body of the chapter is very long, and I felt that a conclusion of all approaches is better off in the general conclusion. Of course, every section within the chapter is closed with a conclusion in order to summarize the respective subfield; only the general conclusion is found in Chap. 5.

4.1 Propositional Systems Without Background Theory

Approaches of this class assume that service operations are functionally specified either through their inputs and outputs or in terms of propositional preconditions and postconditions. Correspondingly, the goal is either to derive a set of desired outputs from a given set of inputs or to find a composition that guarantees a desired (propositional) postcondition to hold when invoked on a given precondition. The first case is simply a special case of the second one, interpreting the inputs $\{i_1, \ldots, i_m\}$ and outputs $\{o_1, \ldots, o_n\}$ of operations as propositions that are conjunctively connected. Note that inputs and outputs sometimes refer to *names* of the data ports and sometimes to the *types* of data ports, but this difference is irrelevant for the composition process.

Given this type of operation specification, we can create propositional planning actions in linear time. For every service operation o_i, we create exactly one planning action a_i. The precondition of a_i corresponds either to the conjunction of inputs or to the precondition of o_i, depending on the type of operation. Likewise, the postcondition of a_i corresponds either to the conjunction of outputs or to the postcondition of o_i, depending on the type of operation. The state space is defined by the powerset of the set of all propositions induced by inputs, outputs, preconditions, or postconditions occurring in the description of any operation.

The number of approaches presented in this section should not hide the fact that most of them solve problems that are trivial or at least very simple. If we assume that the operators are given in advance—and we are not aware of an approach that does not make this assumption—we can create look-up tables in a preprocessing step that allows us to answer queries in constant time. But even if we do not apply such a preprocessing step, most of the composition problems are still solvable within polynomial runtime. This is simply because every service is contained at most once in a composition. Of course, if operations have negative preconditions or postconditions, or if the goal is to find solutions that optimize QoS-properties, the hardness of the underlying problem increases. However, most approaches considered here do not take these aspects into account and, hence, address extremely simple and practically largely irrelevant problems.

4.1.1 IO-Based Composition

Approaches discussed in this section rely only on the *names* or the *types* of parameters of operations. Service operations are not expected to have semantic annotations in terms of preconditions or postconditions. The planning actions can be defined straight forward. For every service operation, there is one action with preconditions corresponding to the names or types of the inputs and positive postconditions corresponding to the names or types of the outputs. The actions do not have negative postconditions.

4.1.1.1 Forward Search

Thakkar et al. propose a naive forward chaining approach to solve the problem [149]. Given the set of available inputs AI, they iteratively add every service operation to the composition whose inputs are a subset of AI and add the outputs of that operation to AI. The process terminates if all required outputs are contained in AI or if all service operations have been added to the composition. However, the unguided forward chaining implies that the composition also contains service operations that are completely irrelevant for obtaining the desired outputs. Nonfunctional properties are also not considered.

Blake and Cummings add the notion of service level agreements (SLA) to the simple composition algorithm [24]. Considered measurements are up-time (reliability), service rate (execution duration + communication time), maintenance (time that the service must announce its downtime before service is disabled), cost, and renegotiation (time before agreement must be renegotiated). The input of the composition algorithm is a set of provided input parameters, required output parameters, and a vector with bounds for the SLA features. The composition algorithm first performs a forward search in order to identify possible workflows. Every workflow satisfies the SLA bounds of the user and transforms the given inputs into the required outputs. Out of the set of candidates, they then choose the workflow that is best with respect to predefined *priorities* among the SLA measurements. While the technical quality of the approach is rather poor, e.g., the description of the composition routine is significantly flawed, the approach brings some new interesting nonfunctional properties that are not considered by other approaches. However, the discussion of related work is quite insufficient. For example, the difference to Zeng et al. is not only the type of considered nonfunctional properties but that the composition is not based on a template but on a search algorithm. Summarizing, the approach is weak from the functional point of view but provides some interesting nonfunctional properties that are not considered by others.

4.1.1.2 Backward Search

Wu et al. address the same setting as Thakkar et al. but address it through backward chaining using a distance-based heuristic [162]. The basic search algorithm is a backward search algorithm that starts at s^* and prepends operations to the current plan; the state resulting from a prepend step is the old state minus the outputs of the prepended operation plus the inputs of the prepended operation. The algorithm stops when the empty state has been reached. This is a formal flaw, because this is usually impossible, and the algorithm should terminate when a subset of s_0 is reached. The choice of operators to be prepended is driven by a heuristic computed in a preprocessing step. Ironically, the heuristic cannot be computed efficiently, because it already explores the whole search space. Apart from that, it is unclear why a heuristic is needed at all for this unduly simple problem.

Another approach of this section is presented by Matskin et al. [95]. The concrete composition algorithm is not even described, but the requests are of the same type as in the case of [149]. There seems to be no relevant novelty.

Pu et al. perform composition based on complex input and output types [125]. The difference to the above approaches is that inputs and outputs are not only described by atomic parameter names but by complex data types as used in XML schema. Given the lack of semantics, which is already a conceptual shortcoming of the simple problems described above, this approach must be considered almost absurd. The main problem of the syntactical approaches, namely that the human must check the proposed solutions if they are semantically valid, is much worse in this setting, because the semantics faults are harder to track. For example, we could require a type *MyClient(cname,transaction[0,*])* that contains the client name and a list of her transactions based on the two types *Client(cname)*. There are two services: The first receives a *Client* and returns the associated *Employee*. The second accepts *Employee[0,*]* and returns the last *transaction* that was approved by every employee listed in the input. The algorithm provided by Pu et al. finds a solution that determines the employee of the client and creates a list only with this employee. This list is passed to the second service, which delivers a transaction, which is again inserted into a new list of transactions (of length 1). Then, a new complex type is created, together with the client name from the beginning and the list of transactions. Now the resulting type contains a list of transactions, but it contains all the transactions that were approved by the employee associated with the client, which is obviously not what was originally intended. The usage of a cost measure slightly alleviates this problem, but the general problem remains.

4.1.1.3 Dependency Graph-Based Approaches

There are a number of approaches based on the so-called dependency graphs. The idea of dependency graphs is to capture relations among services within a graph structure, which is then used to construct a composition.

Initial Models

First Brogi et al. present an approach that considers ontological matchmaking [29]. The initial situation s_0 and the goal situation s^* are sets of desired ontological concepts, e.g., *username* or *address*. First, their algorithm creates a *dependency graph* (DG) that consists of data nodes N_D and process nodes N_P. Combined with the concepts in s_0 (s^* respectively), the data nodes N_D constitute a set I (O respectively) of usable (required) data. For the creation of the dependency graph, they iteratively run a matching algorithm that identifies services that can either work with the data in I or provide at least one element of O. This matching step considers not only exact matches, but also subsuming types, e.g., services are also selected if they require a more general type than the one available. For every matching service, the algorithm adds one process node for the service (unless it is already inserted) and one data node for every input and output concept of the service that is not part of the graph already. It then adds an edge from the nodes of the input concepts to the respective process node and edges from the process node to the nodes of its outputs, respectively. This process ends when no more service can be inserted into the dependency graph. Second, it constructs a concrete composition from the dependency graph by first determining the relevant processes using backward chaining and then, out of this set, computing a sequence of "firable" processes; that is, it creates a sequence of services that can be invoked with the given inputs and that obtain the desired outputs.

While there is some novelty in the construction of a dependency graph, the improvement compared to simple backward chaining seems to be rather slim. The novelty of the dependency graph is that it defines a structure in a preprocessing step that then helps avoid decisions during the search process that would yield dead ends. The absence of quality values makes it hard to qualify different solutions, so the qualitative advantage or disadvantage compared to simple backward chaining or forward chaining is not clear. Given the little relevance of the setting due to the lack of semantics, however, there is no gain in going into a more detailed discussion about this point.

Almost at the same time, a similar approach was presented by Hashemian et al. [54, 55]. Instead of having data nodes and process nodes, the dependency graph in their approach has only data nodes, and there is an edge between node v_1 and v_2 if at least one service has v_2 as an output and requires v_1 as an input; the service may also require more inputs and produce more outputs. The edge is labeled with the *set* of services that satisfy this property. The query is defined by a set of pairs of input and output concepts, which are called dependencies; in [55], a query is a pair of *sets* of inputs and outputs, respectively. For each such pair and for every output concept in the pair, the algorithm searches for a path from the inputs to the respective output concept. An additional feature considered in [55] is the cardinality of inputs and outputs; that is, it can be defined that two objects of a particular type are needed instead of only declaring that "some" object of that type is needed.

There are some difficulties with the way how Hashemian et al. make use of the dependency graph. First, the introduction of cardinalities does make sense in this setting. More precisely, it does not matter if a service requires one object of the type *city*, two such objects, or any other constant number. Once it is clear that at least one such object is needed by a service, we need a plan of how to achieve it. But when we have this plan, it can be used arbitrarily often again to produce further objects of that type (which simply yields two equal objects). Second, the composition approach presented by Hashemian et al. is also unsound in that compositions which may contain services whose inputs are not completely provided. For example, if we want to get from concept a to concept b and there is a service that has two inputs a and a' and needs both to produce b. Then their approach will return the service as a solution, because it defines an edge between a and b in the dependency graph. The fact that some other object a' is required may be encoded in the label but is not relevant in the path finding problem; this requirement is simply omitted. Summarizing, their approach is hardly suitable for solving the tackled problem.

A third approach at that time considering something like a dependency graph was presented by Liu et al. [88]. Here, a structure called "deduced network" is computed in order to determine the possible compositions. The novelty here is that execution prices are considered. However, the quality of this approach is rather poor, because they compute a composition for each output separately and then consider all possible combinations of solutions for the individual subgoals. Among these, they choose the composition with the optimal cost, but it is for example not clear, whether the same service counts twice.

Extended Models

Akkiraju et al. apply an hybrid search to solve the composition problem [5]. The algorithm receives a set of services, a set of provided concepts, and a set of required concepts. First, it computes which services may be relevant for a solution through backward search. Using the remaining services, they then perform a forward search that is guided by a heuristic that is not explained. The approach does basically the same as the algorithm presented by Brogi et al. [29]. Even though it considers ontological concepts in the evaluation of the quality of a solution, the relations among the concepts and their similarities are apparently not considered in the search process itself. Hence, there is no significant novelty in this approach.

Zhou et al. solve the composition problem based on binary trees that encode the dependencies among services [170]. The basis of the computation is a so-called *complete service invocation tree*. Based on this tree, other data structures are derived in order to find a composition. There is no significant novelty in the approach over earlier approaches; in particular, nonfunctional properties are not considered. Since relevant-related work is practically not discussed (in fact, none of the formerly discussed approaches within this section is mentioned), I cannot identify any novelty.

Bouillet et al. describe an approach that solves the same problem as the approaches discussed by Akkiraju et al. [27, 28]. The difference is merely terminological, because they refer to concepts as tags. Even though they claim to use an ontology and to consider subtypes, the planning algorithm used has no native support for this background knowledge, and it is not explained how this knowledge is provided to the planner. Hence, we do not know if and how the type hierarchy can really be considered in the composition process. The discussion of related work (only Lécué et al. and Akkiraju et al. are discussed) does not reveal a significant novelty neither.

Degeler et al. propose an approach that considers the response time of a composition as a nonfunctional criterion [45]. The underlying model is not explicitly called dependency graph, but it has a very similar semantics to the one discussed above. By a simple forward search in the set of possible data flows among services, they determine the minimum response time that any composition has that reaches a particular concept. Then, they apply a backward search individually for each concept to get the "cheapest" composition for the respective concept. The approach brings no novelty and is significantly flawed. First, the approach is not sound, because the backward search does not consider the case that there are no services that can produce required inputs of a service used to provide a goal concept. Second, the model they use assumes that one creates n compositions if n concepts are desired and that these are all executed in parallel. However, this is not a reasonable composition model, in particular given other nonfunctional properties such as price.

Another solution to this problem was proposed by Blanco et al. [25]. They construct a dependency graph quite similar to the one proposed by Brogi et al. [29] but use the notion of Petri nets instead. The innovation is that they consider transactional properties at a risk level as proposed by El Haddad et al. [50]. The difference to El Haddad et al. is that no template is given, but that the composition algorithm tries to find a composition that transforms a set of given input concepts into a set of required output concepts. Some nonfunctional properties (number of service instances, execution time) are considered through constraints (no optimization). As discussed in Sect. 4.1.2, Petri nets are a quite unsuitable model for service composition. They avoid the mentioned problems by not consuming markings from the inputs places when firing transitions, but then one wonders why they use Petri nets at all. Summarizing, the consideration of transactional properties is a novelty, but the model used in the approach is not convincing and the overall problem of finding compositions for concept transformation is still rather irrelevant.

4.1.1.4   Application of GraphPlan

The first one to apply the GraphPlan algorithm [26] to this type of composition problem were Rahmani et al. [126]. The basic idea seems to be that the search process is guided by the distance of the nonfunctional properties to the initial solution. However, the composition algorithm is not described in detail, and, in general, the formalism of the paper is significantly flawed. It is not clear how the nonfunctional properties can be reasonably connected with a heuristic for functionality. Apart from that, given the simplicity of the problem, it is also unclear why a heuristic is needed at all.

Yan et al. proposed a modified version of the standard planner GraphPlan that considers QoS-properties of actions in order to solve the problem [165, 166]. In the modified version, every action node is associated with the cost-properties of the respective action and each proposition node is associated with an optimistic estimate of the costs necessary to produce it. The idea of applying GraphPlan in this setting is somewhat awkward, because the actions do not have negative postconditions, so the heart of GraphPlan, which are the mutexes, are not required. So, approach model does not exploit the strength of GraphPlan but inherits its rather complicated planning process; this even forces them to add a solution reduction algorithm. Moreover, the computation of costs is not reasonable, because they assume the cost for a proposition p to be the cost of the action that produces p plus the maximum cost among the properties within the precondition of the action. But taking the maximum here is not correct, because if the propositions in the preconditions of an action are achieved by several independent operations, only the cost of one of them is considered. Summarizing, Yan et al. add two QoS-properties to the composition model but unnecessarily complicate this actually which is very simple problem.

Recently, Zou et al. have added QoS-properties and preferences to the composition model [171, 172]. The input of the algorithm is a set of service operations, a set of input parameter names, a set of output parameter names, a set of QoS bounds, and weights for the QoS-properties. A service operation w has a set of input names I_w, output names O_w, and values for the QoS-properties Q_w. The set of query input variable names are the initial state s_0, and the query output variable names are the goal situation s^*. A service operation is applicable in a state s iff $I_w \subseteq s$, and the state resulting from the application is $s' = s \cup O_w$. A solution is a sequence of operations such that the obtained state is a superset of s^*. The QoS-properties are aggregated like in [167], and, among the set of valid solutions, the one that optimizes the weighted QoS-aggregation is chosen.

4.1.2 Composition with Preconditions and Effects

Approaches within this section rely on operations that are described in terms of propositional preconditions and postconditions (maybe in addition to inputs and outputs). Hence, for each operation o, we can simply create a planning action a with the same precondition and postcondition. Except ASTRO, all the approaches are monotonic, which means that operations have only positive postconditions; that is, the postcondition only contains positive literals. In ASTRO, operations are part of state transition systems, so the ability of an operation to be fired must be encoded using state literals, which must be negatable. The four paradigms.

4.1.2.1 Constructive Theorem Proving

In [79], Sven Lämmermann proposed an approach to service composition based on so called *meta-interfaces*. The rough idea of meta-interfaces seems to be that they define functionalities (called axioms) in terms of typed variables or constants. A functionality is encoded in terms of propositional logical preconditions and postconditions. A precondition may contain variable names, logical propositions, and subtasks, which are basically lambda-functions that must be solved first. It is satisfied if each of the mentioned variables are known to have been initialized with a value, if the logical propositions are known to be true, and if the subtask has been resolved. The postcondition may contain a variable name, propositions, or an exception; these may be joint also by a disjunctive operator. Given these meta-interfaces, a set of logical rules can be derived. The query fed to the theorem prover is then as follows: Given the rules obtained from the meta-interfaces and a set of variables that is assumed to be set, can we infer that a particular variable can be set?

The two relevant features that most of the other approaches in this section do not have are subtasks and conditional postconditions. Other approaches in this section describe a service with a set of inputs, a set of outputs, preconditions, and postconditions; preconditions and postconditions are conjunctions of propositional atoms. In contrast, Lämmermann allows for subtasks to contain in the preconditions. A subtask itself is also described in terms of preconditions and postconditions, so it can alternatively be seen as an additional input of the type of a lambda-function. Hence, to invoke the respective operation it is not necessary to provide an object of a particular type but a function that implements the specified functionality. The second feature is the possibility of disjoint postconditions of operations, which allows for exception handling. This forces the composition algorithm to pursue alternative execution runs of the composition it is creating. The resulting compositions reflect this feature by containing exception handling or conditional statements.

Compared to the enormous formal corpus that is introduced to describe the approach, the overall benefit is rather small. As for all approaches within this section, the semantic power of the queries that can be sent to the system is quite small. How interesting can it be to determine whether or not a particular variable can be set? Of course, if we would impose constraints on the properties of the object that we set to a variable, the issue would be more interesting, but this is never the case. The low semantics are an issue of all the approaches discussed in this section, but most of them are very easy to understand while the description of this solution is very complex and little comprehensive in many aspects. For example, the description of meta-interfaces with the variables, constants, subtasks, and axioms is little comprehensive when compared with the simple IOPE models that underly the other approaches discussed below.

4.1.2.2   Classical Search Algorithms

Kona et al. present and approach for automated service composition that includes propositional log [74, 75]. They provide a naive forward search algorithm that reminds one of the work of Thakkar et al. [149]. The two additional features to Thakkar are conditions and ontological concepts, but none of them is really considered in a convincing way. Conditions are only sets of propositions, so there is actually no relevant difference between inputs and conditions for the algorithm. Second, ontological concepts are mentioned but not used in an appropriate manner. More precisely, the subsumes-relation is used on sets of inputs, for which it is not defined. Also, neither the algorithm nor the examples show the usage of any ontological subsumption reasoning. Apart from this, the forward chaining-specific problem of incorporating useless services is not resolved at all, so the solutions will usually also contain many services that are irrelevant for the respective query. Summarizing, the approach brings no relevant improvement compared to earlier attempts.

For the same setting, Sheshagiri et al. propose a backward chaining algorithm [135]. The critics are the same as for Kona et al. except the use of backward-chaining. Using backward-chaining at least saves Sheshagiri et al. from constructing compositions that contain irrelevant service operations. However, the distinction between inputs and preconditions on one hand, and outputs and postconditions on the other hand is obsolete in this form. So the overall model is quite similar to the ones discussed above and brings no actual novelty.

Agarwal et al. developed a system called Synthy that adds contingency planning and QoS-properties to the above-explained approaches [1, 2]. The algorithm has a logical composition phase, which creates an abstract workflow, and a so-called physical composition phase, where the abstract workflow is instantiated taking into account the nonfunctional properties. Unfortunately, the logical composition phase is not described sufficiently; they only say that they use limited contingency planning, but it is impossible to figure out how this actually works. The second phase then applies a simplified version of the QoS-optimization model proposed by Zeng et al. [167]. Summarizing, the approach is conceptually relevant due to the integration of planning and QoS, but the formal depth is so low that it is impossible to build upon it.

4.1.2.3 Approaches Based on Resource Models

There are basically two approaches that build on the idea that service composition makes use of resources that are processed. The first is based on Petri nets while the second is based on linear logic. I discuss the two approaches in detail.

Petri Nets

Narayanan et al. were the first to introduce Petri nets to model the consumption and production of data in a service composition [113]. The idea is that the set of all services is encoded as a Petri net, and the task is to find a sequence of transition activations that transforms the initial marking into a goal marking. The Petri net is constructed as follows. For each service operation, there is one transition in the network, and there is one place for every possible assertion over the world (logical atom) and every variable name that is an input or output of a service operation. There is a link between a place and a transition if the assertion or the variable belonging to the place is an input or a precondition of the operation. Likewise, there is a link between a transition and a place if the assertion is an output or an postcondition atom of the operation. The concrete query defines the markings of the network in the beginning. The composition problem is to find a sequence of transition activations such that a given goal marking is reached. Note that, even though the behavior is expressed in situation calculus, it is de facto ground to propositional logic, which is why I discuss it within this section. Later, similar approaches have been proposed by other authors.

Linear Logic

Rao et al. proposed a resource-based approach through the notion of linear logic [77, 127, 128, 129]. A linear logic formula is syntactically similar to propositional logic only that it uses the junctors $\otimes$, $\oplus$, $\multimap$ instead of $\wedge$, $\vee$, $\rightarrow$, respectively. The semantics of $A \otimes B$ is that both resources are available, and $A \oplus B$ means that one of the two is available. $\alpha \multimap \beta$ means that the resources are consumed as described in α and new resources are produced as specified in β. In contrast to propositional logic, a proposition may be contained several times in a conjunction or disjunction in order to express how often the respective information is contained. Services have inputs, which are consumed on execution, and outputs, which are produced after execution. In the descriptions, the functional and nonfunctional parts are separated, but this distinction is not relevant in the formal model or for the solver.

Required but nonconsumed properties must be modeled by being both consumed and produced by a service. So similar to the other approaches discussed in this section, the query defines provided inputs and nonfunctional properties/resources on one hand and desired outputs and demanded nonfunctional properties on the other hand. A (very limited built-in) background theory allows to count the resources available and prevents that more resources than available are used.

Discussion of Resource-Based Composition

In spite (or perhaps because) of the attention they gained in the community, we should make clear that these models are substantially unsuitable for the problem of service composition. While the applied modeling techniques may be interesting in industrial manufacturing systems, digital data, which are the resources of interest here, cannot be considered as consumable units. Once a piece of information is created, it can be used arbitrarily often *without* being consumed; there is simply no need to keep track of the *number* of objects available of a particular type. This is the same objection I already discussed for the approach of Hashemian et al. The only acceptable argument given in [127] is the application of these techniques to nonfunctional properties such as budget; for example, the budget is 20 EUR and every service consumes a certain amount of the budget. However, putting these nonfunctional properties on one level with the functional properties, which are also consumed and against any intuition cannot be used for a second time, yields a quite inappropriate and unnecessarily complex model. Even if it is possible to avoid the consumption semantics in individual cases by declaring every input also as an output, this yields a very unnatural and blown up model.

4.1.2.4 Abduction-Based Service Composition

Okutan et al. propose a composition algorithm based on logical *abduction* [115, 118]. In logical abduction, we assume some knowledge base α and an observation β as given, and we are interested in an explanation γ such that $\alpha \wedge \gamma \models \beta$ holds. In the case of service composition, the formula α is a conjunction of service operation encodings (e.g., in terms of rules) and an initial situation, β encodes what shall be known for the outputs of the composition. The task of the composition algorithm is to find the formula γ, which encodes the *application* of service operations. Intuitively, the service descriptions (α) together with the information how the services are used γ explains how the desired outputs β are obtained. In order to cope with the problem that knowledge is bound to *situations*, Okutan et al. use the event calculus to encode the knowledge and the services.

The idea of modeling the composition task as an abduction problem is intuitive and may be an interesting option, but the approach is still quite preliminary and need substantial improvement in order to be comparable with the other FOL-based approaches discussed below. Even though this is not a general limitation of the abductive approach, it is currently restricted to propositional logical preconditions and postconditions. Only one problem arising from this limitation is that a type-hierarchical evaluation of parameters is not possible. For example, an object of the type employee cannot be used as an input for a service that requires an object of the type person, even though if employee is a subtype of person. There is a basic support for nonfunctional properties (execution duration, price, reliability, availability), but the model is rather poor. For example, increasing costs increase the score of compositions while they should decrease it, and there is no weighting of the qualities. Summarizing, the abduction-based approach presented in [115] is an interesting initial work but still needs several improvements in order to be on the same level as the FOL-based approaches discussed below.

One significant advantage of the abduction-based approach is that it is directly apt for partial ordered composition. That is, the abductive reasoner does not create a totally ordered composition but only fixes the data flow, which defines a partial order on the service invocations. This property reduces the search space size significantly.

4.1.2.5 The ASTRO Approach

Probably inspired by the Roman model, Traverso, Pistore, and Bertoli developed a composition algorithm that considers services as finite automata [23, 121, 122, 123, 151]. The inputs of the composition algorithm are a finite set of finite state automata, which correspond to the existing services, and a *set* S^* of accepted (and possibly ranked) goal states. In ASTRO, the state of a service is a conjunction of *propositional logical* atoms encoding the values of its variables. The state of the considered system as a whole is defined as the product of states of the services; the initial state s_0 is implicitly defined through the product of initial states of the services. The composition algorithm must construct a *controller* that drives the whole system into any of the goal states of S^* by exchanging messages with the services and, thereby, changing their state and the state of the system as a whole. A particular challenge in this setting is that the automata that model the services are not generally deterministic, so the controller must be able to cope with nondeterministic evolvements of the environment it interacts with.

The two main differences to other approaches within this section are the consideration of constraints on the invocation of service operations and the nondeterminism of those operations. For example, the request for the availability of a product could be true or false; while other approaches subsumes these two responses under a type definition, the ASTRO model considers them on the value level (in form of different response messages). These are important aspects, because both of them impose a significant increase of the computational complexity. In fact, one could model the services of the ASTRO model simply as one planning operation and encode the source and target states in the preconditions and postconditions. For example, suppose that a service has a transition t from state s to states $\{s_1', \ldots, s_n'\}$, then t is an operation of the service, and we could encode it as a planning action in set theory with preconditions s, positive postconditions $s_1' \vee \cdots \vee s_n'$, and negative postconditions *s*. So we can understand the addressed problem as a nondeterministic variant of the other approaches within this section.

Similar to the discussion on the Roman model, my main objections against this approach is the rather low benefit of automation measured as the ratio between specification effort and achievement of automation. First, the user of the ASTRO framework must specify the goal states *in terms of states of services*. In other words, the user has already resolved the *selection problem* by deciding which services are part of the final composition; no other approach makes this assumption. Note that this also makes the consideration of nonfunctional properties obsolete, which are never a topic within the ASTRO framework. Second, the user must not only solve the selection problem but also know the admissible final states of those services and design the query such that it leaves the system in a consistent state. Third, the data flow is not considered in the automatization process, and the user must specify it in advance; in particular, the user must say which inputs of a service are read from which outputs of which other service. Having the data flow completely encoded this way, the parameters occurring in the operations of the services are fixed, and the communication with the services can be understood as sending and receiving parameter-less *signals*. The remaining problem is to find a *tree* that reflects the possible signals exchanged by the controller and the service community. While this problem may or may not be hard to solve from a computational point of view, the user is certainly faster in simply writing the software than to specify all these details for then having the algorithm automate a tiny part of the task.

Apart from these utility objections, there is also a problem with the soundness of the approach. This can seen best in the latest variant [23], which summarizes the efforts of the earlier attempts. The problem is that the controller may invoke service operations with data that is not available. For example, it may request the *shipper* service for an offer for a package of some size *before* the *producer* service is invoked to determine the size. This is possible, because the requirement definition only defines the partners between the data must flow, but there are no restrictions on the availability.

Huai et al. presented an approach based on the ASTRO model that applies query-based learning to solve the composition problem [61]. Similar to the Eagle language developed by Traverso et al., they use computational tree logic (CTL) to encode the composition problem. However, the approach differs from the above one only in the algorithm that solves the problem, so the major critics discussed above hold likewise.

Summarizing, the ASTRO project enhances the propositional-based composition by *conditional branches* and by a service model that considers *usage restrictions* on service operations, but its utility for the user is little convincing. Of course, the consideration of protocols that limit the way how services are invoked is an important feature. Also, the integration of different possible outcomes of service invocations into the controller is an improvement; in fact, these are equivalent to *if-then-else* constructs. Unfortunately, the way how the user requirements are specified is little convincing, and it is not clear why the user should ever make the effort to provide all these formal specifications. However, these two aspects are not necessarily tied together. One can envision a framework that takes the underlying service model used in ASTRO but works with a different form of requirement definitions.

4.1.3 Concluding Discussion

Table 4.1 summarizes the approaches discussed so far in this section. It shows whether or not an approach considers nonfunctional properties and whether compositions may contain diverging control flows (if-statements in the control flow). Loops are generally not considered by the approaches in this class. I do not distinguish between the actual information that is encoded (parameters or preconditions and postconditions), because this has no effect on the algorithm. The semantics of these propositions is either "a datum of some type x is available" or "some condition c is true", but actually the first assertion is only a special case of the second.

In spite of the number of approaches in this subclass, the relevance of the problem addressed here is quite small. There are two major concerns about most approaches within this section, which I discuss in the following.

First, the problem is technically so simple that the need to invent a new composition algorithm is quite unclear. Unless nonfunctional properties are considered, the composition task can be simply encoded using PDDL and be solved extremely fast using standard planners, which makes many approaches obsolete [5, 28, 29, 54, 75, 95, 135, 149, 162, 171].

Second, the practical relevance of most of the approaches is very small due to the almost complete absence of semantic information. Except for the ASTRO project that almost specifies the whole solution in advance, the description of desired behavior is highly insufficient. Consider that we have a composition problem where we provide an input *Position* and an output *Telephone Number*. There are numerous possibilities for the semantic connection between the desired telephone number and the position. It could be the phone number of the house closest to the position, the number of the mobile phone that most recently called from that position, the number of a local taxi company, the number of an employee responsible for the respective area around the position, etc. It is highly questionable that the composition algorithm returns a composition that realizes the desired semantic relation.

Probably involuntarily, Hashemian et al. show that the semantics of this composition model becomes quite absurd in the case that operations need more than one input of the same type. For example, they suggest a service operation that computes the distance between two cities, i.e. the operation requires two city objects as inputs. However, the composition algorithm has no reason to provide two *different* cities to that operation, and, in fact, their approach simply copies the solution to get the first city to provide the second city, so the objects will be (always) the same. This example shows in a very illustrative way that these propositional techniques can be hardly considered more than heuristics for FOL composition algorithms discussed above that can compute solutions of a relaxed model fast.

Table 4.1 Overview of approaches without a given structure that rely only on parameter names or propositional conditions

Name	QoS	Alt	Particular Strengths	Particular Weaknesses
Thakkar et al.	○	○	-	compositions contain irrelevant operations
Blake et al.	●	○	consideration of service level agreements	formally flawed
Wu et al.	○	○	-	formally weak
Matskin et al.	○	○		poor formal model
Pu et al.	○	○	considers complex types	semantic gaps are even harder to track
Brogi et al.	○	○	good formal model	poor semantics, no ontological matching
Hashemian et al.	○	○	-	poor semantics, unsound algorithm
Liu et al.	●	○	clear algorithm description	poor semantics, inefficient algorithm
Akkiraju et al.	○	○	good evaluation	no novelty
Zhou et al.	○	○	-	poor formal model, no novelty
Bouillet et al.	○	○		reinvents terminology, no novelty
Degeler et al.	●	○	transactional properties	unreasonable assumptions, unsound
Blanco et al.	●	○		Petri net based model
Rahmani et al.	●	○	considers user preferences	formally flawed
Yan et al.	●	○	-	unnecessarily complex, conceptually flawed
Zou et al.	●	○		no semantics
Lämmermann	○	●	functions as inputs	unnecessarily complicated model
Kona et al.	○	○	consideration of rudimentary conditions	insufficiently formalized, forward chaining
Sheshagiri et al.	○	○	no irrelevant services in solutions	poor novelty compared to I/O-approaches
Agarwal et al.	●	●	-	insufficiently formalized
Narayanan et al.	○	●	-	consumption-based model
Rao et al.	●	●		consumption-based model
Pistore et al.	○	●	usage constraints, non-determinism	automated task very small
Huai et al.	○	●	usage constraints, non-determinism	automated task very small
Okutan et al.	○	○	uses special calculi (event calculus & abduction)	initial stage, QoS model flawed

QoS = Quality of Service (NF-Properties), *Alt* = Compositions with alternative control flows (if-statements)

● = approaches substantially support the particular class, ○ = approaches partially support the particular class. The rows within the table correspond to the order in which the approaches were discussed. The *double lines* separate the approaches discussed in different subsections from each other. Literature references can be found in the respective discussions of the approaches

The two positively remarkable properties addressed by some approaches of this subclass are the potential *nondeterminism* of operations and the idea of *partial ordered planning* through abduction. Nondeterminism is considered by Lämmermann [79] (through the notion of exceptions) and in the ASTRO project [23]. That is, the composition algorithm must take into account that the invocation of an operation may have several results, and it must find a solution for each of these outcomes. Abduction is sketched by Okutan et al. [115], which is highly interesting due to the partial ordering of operations. Searching for compositions that are only partially ordered greatly simplifies the search space. However, none of these characteristics compensate the shortcomings of the low semantics imposed by the purely propositional preconditions and postconditions.

4.2 Propositional Systems with Background Theory

The only difference between this subclass and the previously discussed one is that there is some kind of background knowledge that must be encoded in addition to the service operations themselves. The most relevant case is the encoding of a type hierarchy, which is discussed in Sect. 4.2.1. For example, one service determines the price of a product in EUR and another service accepts currency objects as input. Now we have the knowledge that every amount in EUR is also a currency value, hence $EUR(x) \rightarrow Currency(x)$. Hence, we would expect that the second service can be run with the output of the first one. However, approaches discussed above cannot connect these two services based on the type hierarchy information.

Again, since approaches in this section only ever ask for the derivation of *some* object of a given type, we do not need the predicate calculus version of the knowledge base. For example, we can rewrite the above rule simply as $EUR \rightarrow Currency$, meaning that "whenever we have some object of type EUR, we also have an object of type Currency". These propositional rules can then be simply encoded as additional planning actions.

The concept of simple type hierarchies can be generalized by the idea of similarity matching. Instead of saying that the output of an operation o_1 can be used as input of operation o_2 if it is as least as specific as the respectively required input type, a similarity function is used instead to decide whether or not the object can be passed in that way. So similarity matching is somewhat a semantic generalization of the strict type hierarchy. In particular, we could have a similarity measure that takes into account several ontologies and tries to match them based on lexical comparisons. Composition approaches that support this type of background knowledge are discussed in Sect. 4.2.2.

From the complexity viewpoint, approaches using similarity functions are slightly more complex to encode as a propositional logical planning problem. The reason is that the similarity function encodes the rules that are needed to represent the concept compatibilities *implicitly*. Computing the existence of such a rule for every pair of concepts requires quadratic time in the number of concepts. However, this translation can still be considered efficient.

4.2.1   Composition with Type Hierarchies

4.2.1.1   Classical Backward Search

A simple backward greedy search was proposed by Weise et al. [161]. The type
hierarchy matching is hidden in the implementation of a predicate called "Promising".
Compositions are simply ordered by some heuristic c, where c "combines the size
of the set unsatisfied parameters, the composition lengths, the number of satisfied
parameters, and the number of known concepts". The simplicity of this solution
underlines once more the trivial problem character.

The approaches published by Bartalos and Bieliková are based on a simple backward chaining algorithm [15]. The algorithm is based on a predefined graph that
defines which services provide data required by other services. This idea is similar
to the dependency graph proposed in [29, 54]. In contrast to some other approaches
in this section, it considers the ontological type hierarchy. Later, they published
improved variants of their algorithms that can deal with simple first-order logic constraints (cf. Sect. 4.3.2.4).

In the same year, Talantikite et al. propose a backward chaining algorithm [148].
They claim that they improve earlier approaches [10, 11] (cf. Sect. 4.2.2) with better runtime through a precompiled structure they call semantic network. However,
neither are these claims supported by evaluation nor is the concept of their semantic network sufficiently innovative to constitute a significant improvement; these
networks can be computed efficiently also by other approaches. In contrast, the
approaches in [10, 11] actually do consider similarity that exceed mere type systems, while Talantikite et al. only consider exact matches and subsumption matches.
The approach also considers some nonfunctional properties (exec-time, resource
consumption) by ordering solutions according to a predefined preference function.
Hence, the approach provides a composition algorithm and some consideration of
nonfunctional properties that we were missing in the work of Constantinescu et al.
but it brings no significant improvement compared to existing solutions.

Later, Rodriguez-Mier et al. presented a composition technique that performs a
heuristic backward search based on a layered dependency graph [132]. The set of
services is partitioned into layers such that L_i contains the services whose inputs can
be satisfied by the union of outputs of services contained in L_j with $j < i$. The first
and the last layer contain only a dummy service with outputs corresponding to the
request inputs and inputs corresponding to the request outputs respectively. Then, an
A^* algorithm is applied to search backwards for a solution. Every node represents a
set of (ontological) types that must still be achieved, and the root node is the set of
required outputs. For a node n, there is a successor for each set of services whose joint
outputs cover the types described in n; for types not coverable in this way, a dummy
service is introduced that has the same type has an input an defers the decision of
how to obtain it. A node is a solution if it is empty. The overall description and
evaluation of the approach is good, and the used heuristic seems to be admissible. Its
only drawback seems to be that nonfunctional properties are not considered at all.

4.2.1.2 Contingency Search

The earliest works that consider ontological type hierarchies in service composition were presented by Constantinescu et al. [41, 42, 43]. In this approach, inputs and outputs of service operations have a type with a domain. An operation is applicable if, for each input, we have a variable whose domain is a subset of the domain of the input variable; i.e., the input must have a value that is accepted for the input variable. In the ontological context, this is often called the *subsumption* relation, but Constantinescu et al. consider also non-ontological types, which is why the applicability is defined this way. While bringing ontological matchmaking to service composition was a conceptual novelty at time of publication, the overall quality of their contribution is rather thin. The formal model is partially unsound, e.g., in the definition of the plugin match for services and query in [42], and the description of composition algorithms is insufficient; in fact, a formal algorithm is only specified in [41], and it is kept very abstract. Also, planning with disjunctive postconditions is far from being trivial; however, this is not discussed at all. Summarizing, Constantinescu et al. presented the fundament for ontological-based service composition but the composition algorithm itself is not convincing.

4.2.1.3 Genetic Programming Solutions

In the same paper as already discussed above, Weise et al. also propose a genetic algorithm to solve the composition problem [161]. In every iteration, the compositions in the pool are mutated by removing the first service with probability σ or to prepend a new promising service with probability $1 - \sigma$; a heuristic is used as a fitness function. Little surprisingly, the runtime of this technique (that frequently revokes its own decisions) is much slower than the one of the simple search techniques.

Rodriguez-Mier et al. presented an approach that randomly mutates programs based on a genetic algorithm [133]. The basis of the algorithm is a simple process grammar that defines the language of all admissible programs. The fact that they exchange control structures completely at random (e.g., replace an if-statement with a parallel execution or vice versa) almost surely yields tons of absurd compositions. Of course, these may produce the desired output types, but the resulting compositions must be expected to be quite unintuitive and semantically unsuitable. Summarizing, the approach is a technique to "gamble" for programs, but the degree of randomness of programs together with the low semantic level renders it completely irrelevant.

4.2.1.4 Hybrid Techniques

Dependency Graph Composition

Jiang et al. present an approach that stores the optimal QoS value for each concept in order to optimize the global QoS value of the resulting composition [63, 64]. Through forward chaining, the algorithm first determines the services that can be executed from the initial situation. Then, it iteratively "triggers" each applicable service and updates the QoS value for each concept that is provided by the respective service. The set of applicable services is extended by the concepts that are outputs of the services already considered. After this procedure, they apply a backward search algorithm to find the best composition with respect to QoS-properties.

Unfortunately, the approach exhibits several significant flaws. Not only is the formal model inconsistent in many parts, also the claim that the algorithm provides globally optimal solutions is false. Suppose for example, that concept a is given and b and c are desired. If there is a service that computes b and c and has cost 3, and there is one service each producing b and c, respectively, with cost 2, then the composition will include the two simple services, because they are the cheapest *local* solutions; however, the costlier service would be better here. Also, the QoS properties are unduly simplified into one single value, and the aggregation of these values remains unclear. Since the comparison to related work is also very thin, there seems to be no significant contribution going along with their approach.

Clustering Approaches

Wagner et al. present an approach based on ontological grouping [159, 160]. The composition algorithm receives a set of services, a type ontology, and a specification of a goal service as input. The algorithm consists of two steps. First, a directed graph is computed where the node set corresponds to the set of services, and there is a link between n_1 and n_2 if the service n_2 *subsumes* the service n_1. Subsumption is defined as follows: Service n_2 subsumes n_1 iff for each input (type) of n_1, n_2 has an equal or more specific input (type), and for each output of n_2, n_1 has an equal or more specific output (type). Intuitively, n_1 can be used whenever n_2 can be used. This process yields a graph with several unconnected node groups; every group has a root, which is called the representative (most general service of the group). Second, a backward chaining algorithm iteratively determines the representative services that contribute to the (remaining) goal and add the corresponding cluster to the plan. If a plan is found that does not have any open inputs anymore, it is marked as a solution. The algorithm checks all possible plans and updates the solution whenever a plan with better "utility" is found; utility here is expressed in terms of reliability and price.

In general, the algorithm leaves a rather weak impression. As so often for approaches in this class, the simplicity of the problem hardly justifies the complicated algorithms. First, the description of the algorithm has several conceptual deficiencies. For example, the algorithm tries *every* possible plan, a strategy that can hardly be considered an improvement for runtime. Second, a composition is a set of *links*, but the algorithm does not at all explain how these links are added to the plan; the complete logic is hidden in an opaque function *computeNextStep*. Third, the approach claims to consider nonfunctional properties, but the QoS model is rather weak. Indeed, the computation of the reliability measure as a "failure among all services within the group" is a good idea, but unfortunately this is the *only* considered property (a formula to compute the price is given but cannot be computed deterministically). Apart from these objections, the service model considers preconditions and postconditions, but these are completely ignored by the algorithm. Summarizing, the approach brings no significant novelty with earlier approaches in the class.

Ma et al. proposed a further approach based on clustering [91]. Services are clustered based on the outputs they produce. Then the clusters are used to compute a possibly appropriate composition, but the paper fails to make clear how this works. The computation is based on a search in a graph that is not formally defined. Hence, it is not possible to verify the soundness or the evaluation of the approach.

4.2.2 Composition with Similarity Matching

An approach based on backward-chaining for types ground in multiple ontologies was presented by Aversano et al. [11]. Going layer-wise, the approach tries in iteration i to find possible sets of services that produce the concepts desired for layer i, where the first layer corresponds to the goal state s^*. Each such set becomes a new node in the search graph, and the algorithm is recursively applied to it. Ontological types of inputs and outputs may stem from different ontologies. In order to determine whether a service produces a desired output, the matchmaking algorithm considers the type name, properties defined on the concept, and the relation to other concepts through the subclass or superclass relation; hence, the matchmaking is not type hierarchical but rather exact matching among possibly different ontologies. The search process is guided by a node evaluation function that is based on nonfunctional properties. The conceptual explanation of the function is reasonable, but a more formal definition would be desirable. Its major weaknesses are that it does not support hierarchical type recognition for types within one ontology, and that the support for nonfunctional properties is rather rudimentary. However, given that it is one of the first approaches in the class, it makes a significant contribution that exceeds the ones made by some of the succinct approaches.

An approach closely related to the dependency graphs explained in the previous section was proposed by Arpinar et al. [10]. The algorithm receives a set of input concepts and output concepts, and it has the task to return a composition that obtains the desired outputs given the inputs. It first determines the similarity for each pair of (o_y, i_x) where o is an output of service operation y and i is an input of a different service operation x. The similarity is computed by their "ontological distance", but it is not explained in detail what this means. The result can be seen as a graph with nodes corresponding to services and with an edge from node y to node x if y has an output o and x has an input i such that the above condition holds. This graph has two distinct nodes, one for the initial situation and one for the goal situation with edges respectively for the query inputs and outputs. Then, for each input of a service, they compute the "shortest distance" for each input starting from the user input; unfortunately, it is not clear what is meant exactly by distance, but it may be the number of edges. Third, for each service, the shortest distance is computed (maximum among all shortest distances among its inputs). Finally, if the shortest distance for the goal node is not infinite, a solution exists (and it has been computed implicitly) during the former algorithm. Even though the approach provides a formal

model, the actual computation of similarity remains rather vague. Also, it is not clear
how the quality of services is considered in the composition process.

In 2006, Lécué and Léger presented a composition algorithm based on so-called
casual link matrices [83]. The general idea of casual link matrices is to store information about which outputs of services can be used as inputs for other services.
The basis for this matrix are casual links between ontological concepts, which make
take values 1 (exact match), $\frac{2}{3}$ (subsumption), $\frac{1}{3}$ (plugin), and 0 if no matching is
possible. For every concept that is the input of any service, the matrix has a row and a
column. In addition, it has a column for each concept contained in the request. A cell
at position i, j contains a set of tuples (x, y) where x may be a service with i among
its inputs and having an output o whose similarity to the concept j is greater than 0.
In addition, x may be the concept j itself to denote that the concept is known; in this
case, y has the value 1. The algorithm $Ra4C$ is supposed to find a solution through
regression-based search, starting from the desired concepts. Intuitively, it figures
out candidate services for the missing goals and, for each candidate, it recursively
invokes itself for the inputs of that candidate.

Unfortunately, the technical quality of the approach is very poor. In general,
the formal part of the paper is not only very complicated but also exhibits several
flaws. For example, the definition of the cells of a casual link matrix is not sound,
and the proof of the theorem on composability (which is should rather have the
status of a proposition) is technically unsound. However, the most crucial flaws are
contained in the composition algorithm itself. While the goals β are always treated
as a *set* of concepts, the algorithm seems to treat them only as a single concept. Also,
the algorithm simply ignores the tuples in the matrix that are defined on concepts
instead of services, which makes one wonder why these were introduced. Another
problem is that the algorithm returns a logical formula where the atoms correspond
to ontological concepts; it is not clear how a service composition can be constructed
from this formula. Summarizing, casual link matrices may introduce an interesting
concept for ontology-based service composition, but the $Ra4C$ algorithm presented
in the paper cannot be considered a suitable solution for the composition problem
addressed in the paper.

In [82], Lécué and Delteil build on top of the $Ra4C$ algorithm in order to only produce robust compositions. The motivation is that the $Ra4C$ algorithm also considers
links between services that are only valid due to subsumption match, which is not
generally sound. For example, it allows to use a person object where an employee is
necessary, given that employee is a subconcept of person. Their approach is based
on the idea that it is possible to specify so called *extra description* for the more general concept to cast it down to the more specific one. They suppose that these extra
descriptions can be computed automatically, but it is not explained how this can be
achieved. Hence, their approach does not constitute a convincing improvement.

Another approach considering similarity was presented by Chifu et al. [39]. The
approach is similar to the ones discussed above, and the only innovation worth being
mentioned is that outputs that cannot be obtained are added as a required input; this
makes the approach a little more robust. This is, however, the only new aspect of

their approach, and none of the related work discussed earlier is mentioned in the paper.

4.2.3 Concluding Discussion

We can briefly summarize these approaches by saying that they consider more technical possibilities of connecting operations but do not resolve the semantic shortcomings discussed in the previous section. That is, the consideration of type hierarchies or similarity functions is a nice additional feature but does not resolve any of the core critics discussed in Sect. 4.1.3. As long as we have no concise description of the *behavior*, which is much more than the types of inputs and outputs even though described through semantic concepts, compositions are mostly unlikely to achieve the desired task.

Note that, apart from this discussion, there could be other types of background knowledge imaginable, but there are no approaches using them. For example, we could imagine knowledge of the form "if service k is used in a composition, then service l may not be used" like applied for the case of template-based composition Sect. 3.2. This type of knowledge could not be directly encoded into the planning problem but would have to remain as a constraint on the meta level. However, I am not aware of any approach that exploits this type of knowledge, and, of course, this would not change anything about the above critics neither (Table 4.2).

4.3 FOL-Based Systems

Approaches of this subclass allow to encode behavior on the level of knowledge about identifiable objects. For example, we may talk about two zip codes and are interested in the distance between the two cities belonging to those zip codes; there will be objects for the zip codes, for the cities, and for the distance, respectively. Forming expressions over objects is enabled by first-order logic (FOL).

I organize the approaches within this class into three further subclasses

1. There are approaches that, similarly to the above techniques, do not relate inputs of operations to their outputs. Still, the behavioral description is more complex, because within the set of inputs and outputs respectively, the objects can be related to each other; that is, preconditions can relate the inputs to each other and postconditions can relate the outputs to each other. Section 4.3.1 discusses approaches of this type.
2. If the postconditions of operations may relate outputs of the operation to inputs, the space of possible compositions is generally *infinite*. Approaches that allow for such postconditions but that make assumptions that avoid infinite search space are discussed in Sect. 4.3.2.

Table 4.2 Overview of approaches without a given structure that rely only on possibly ontological types

Name	TH	Sim	QoS	Alt	Particular Strengths	Particular Weaknesses
Bartalos et al.	●	○	○	○	considers ontological types	very superficial algorithms
Talantikite et al.	●	○	●	○	composition algorithm presented	little innovation
Rodriguez-Mier et al.	●	○	○	○	good formal models	no similarity measures, no QoS
Constantinescu et al.	●	○	○	○	considers ontological types	formally flawed, no concise algorithm
Jiang et al.	●	○	●	○	-	flawed formalism, conceptually unsound
Wagner et al.	●	○	●	○	innovative reliability measure	formally weak, little innovation
Ma et al.	●	○	●	○	-	flawed formalism
Aversano et al.	○	●	●	○	integration of multiple ontologies	minor formal issues, no hierarchy
Arpinar et al.	●	●	●	○	integration of multiple ontologies	superficial algorithm description
Lécué et al. (a)	●	●	○	○	casual link matrices	formally flawed
Chifu et al. (a)	●	●	○	○	concrete algorithms given	no innovation

TH = Hierarchical Type System, *Sim* = Ontological Similarity Matching, *QoS* = Quality of Service (NF-Properties), *Alt* = Compositions with alternative control flows (if-statements)

This table summarizes the discussion of the approaches of this class. The approaches are listed in the order in which the approaches were discussed. The *double lines* separate the approaches discussed in different subsections from each other. Literature references can be found in the respective discussions of the approaches

3. Approaches that consider postconditions that relate inputs and outputs of an operation and that do not limit the potentially infinite search space are discussed in Sect. 4.3.3.

4.3.1 Approaches Without I/O-Relations

The two approaches in this section are similar to the ones discussed in Sects. 4.1 and 4.2 except that preconditions and postconditions can contain relational information referring to the inputs *or* outputs (but not both).

Composition of Relational Concepts

Ambite et al. propose a system for the composition of services where inputs and outputs are relations instead of opaque values [8]. Presumably, the input for the algorithm is a set of services, each of which is described by input and output relations, and a query consisting of a set of input and output relations. I write "presumably", because it is never clearly said what a query is; however, this is the most natural interpretation, which is also shared by Hoffmann et al. [59]. Every relation is factored, which means that it is associated with an ontological concept. The planning algorithm applies partial ordered backward search. It maintains an agenda of concepts that have not been achieved yet. In each step, it identifies a candidate service that has as an output a concept that is equal or more specific than one of the concepts in the agenda. A data link is then added between the inserted service and the service taking the produced output. The innovative point is that the algorithm knows the structure of the relations sent between the services and can perform standard relational algebraic operations such as selection, union, etc., to *synthesize* an input needed by a successor service.

The conceptual aspect of integrating a relational view into service composition is innovative, but the approach only partially delivers on its promises. The actual innovation of the approach is that artificial adapter services can be constructed on the fly in order to translate known relations into desired relations. This is discussed in sufficient detail for the translation obtained by the selection operator of the relational algebra. However, they then claim that they also apply such a mediator algorithms for the operations of projection, union, and join. But it is completely unclear how the presented algorithm translates to these operations; in particular the realization of this mediator for projection and join are far from being straight forward.

Note that there is no semantic relation between inputs and outputs of services. That is, we have a great deal of information about the *structure* of inputs and outputs, but we do not know how the output relations of services relate to the input relations. In this sense, the approach does not provide richer behavioral semantics than the above techniques.

Summarizing, the approach presented by Ambite et al. marks a significant improvement for the application of concept-based composition, but its actual relevance can hardly be judged based on the lack of concise descriptions. On one hand, it allows for mediator-based composition by providing structural information about ontological concepts. This is significantly more than what is possible with any other approach discussed above. On the other hand, the description of the approach is very imprecise on essential questions; e.g., one misses a concise definition of queries accepted by the composition algorithm. Indeed, the formal parts contained in the paper are (for the most part) sound and comprehensive, but the problem is with the parts that are not described. The reader only gets a rough intuition of the inputs and outputs of the composition algorithm, but since they never make an explicit statement, it is not sufficient to reliably classify the capacities of the approach. In particular, the benefit compared to established relational systems, say Prolog, does not become entirely clear.

Planning with Strict Forward Effects

Hoffmann et al. present a composition algorithm based on (conformant) forward search [59, 60, 136]. The algorithm input is a *set* of possible initial states, a desired goal state, a set of service operations that can be applied, and a simple background theory (ontology). Here, a state is a conjunction of ground literals. A service operation o is applicable in a state s with input values X and output values Y iff the objects X are known in s, the output objects are *not* known in s, and if the preconditions of o interpreted under X are contained in s. The requirement that the outputs Y yet do not exist accounts for the idea that the results of each service invocation are stored in new data containers. Using a forward chaining technique, the algorithm extends the current plan with applicable actions. Every node n in the search space is associated with a formula ϕ_n in conjunctive normal form (CNF) that reflects the postcondition of the composition corresponding to it. A candidate n is a solution to the query iff $\phi_n \models s^*$; that is, if the postcondition guarantees that every literal of the goal situation s^* is true.

The approach makes two simplifying assumptions that dismiss the necessity of belief revision. First, every literal in the postconditions of an operation contains at least one output of the operation. This implies that the application of a service operation can never directly produce knowledge that is inconsistent to the former state; this is because every literal contains a constant (of Y) that was not contained in the previous state. Second, it is required that in every clause of the background theory (which is assumed to be in CNF too) the literals share all of the variables, i.e., the variables occurring in a literal are equal for all the literals in a clause. This makes sure that it is also not possible to combine the newly obtained knowledge with the background theory to infer new knowledge that talks only about constants that were already known previously; otherwise, the newly obtained knowledge could yield an implicit contradiction. Problems that satisfy these two properties are said to exhibit *forward effects*.

In order to reduce the number of actions that must be considered, they make another quite serious simplification, which they call *strict* forward effects. The second of the above two conditions is restricted more by requiring that *all* variables occurring in the postconditions of an operation are outputs. The serious consequence of this restriction is that the outputs cannot be related to inputs of the service anymore.

I think that this is assumption is *too* restrictive, but at least this issue is discussed honestly, and the authors also point out that there are still realistic problems that can be solved under this restriction. Under the assumption of strict forward effects, the composition problem is only slightly more expressive than in the propositional systems.

Even though the algorithm uses an (admissible) heuristic, it is highly questionable whether forward search is a good approach for service composition. The key problem of forward search is that it also considers actions that are not relevant for the goal. This problem increases by an order of magnitude in the service composition scenario in which every action creates new objects and, thereby, enables many new actions. In particular, the number of children of each node in the search space increases with each step. It is hardly imaginable that we can get a heuristic that is sufficiently well informed to efficiently guide a best-first search process. Probably, the only hope is to try some hill-climbing strategy and to cut irrelevant elements later on. Of course, in the case of strict forward effects, this problem is relieved by the fact that each operation must be considered at most once. However, in the general case, forward search is probably a borderline hopeless project; their results exhibits enormous search runtimes even for the highly restricted case of strict forward effects.

4.3.2 I/O-Relational Approaches for Finite Spaces

The following approaches describe the behavior of operations by relating the produced outputs to the inputs. The potential infiniteness of the set of compositions is avoided in several ways.

1. The simplest way to make the search space finite is to allow only for compositions that contain an operation at most once.
2. The information integration approach is bound by the fact that all operations work on a *central* data model, which is finite.
3. The approaches applying PDDL bound the model by assuming only a finite number of containers that can be used to pass information among operations.
4. Finally, the technique proposed by Bartalos assumes that the precondition of an operation must completely be satisfied by the preceding operation in the composition, which also bound the set of possible compositions.

4.3.2.1 Limitation of Operation Usage

An approach that makes use of SMT solvers to address the composition problem was presented by Gulwani et al. [53]. Here, the input of the composition algorithm are an input vector, a desired postcondition, and a set of available operations; it is assumed that the composition produces exactly one output whose relation to the inputs is described in the postcondition. Every operation is likewise described by an input vector and its postconditions. The algorithm creates a composition that is a *sequence* of *all* of the available operations. So the composition algorithm (i) determines a permutation of the operations and (ii) fixes the data flow between them. To this end, they introduce so called *local variables* that reflect the position of an operation in the final composition; since every operation has one output, this index also refers to a datum produced by the respective operation. The algorithm then encodes the integrity constraints on the data flow in a formula and passes it to an SMT solver together with the operation descriptions and the desired postcondition. If the solver finds a data flow such that the desired specification must necessarily be satisfied, the respective data flow, (which imposes also the control flow) is returned.

The limitation that it creates compositions that make use of every operation exactly once is a quite strong shortcoming. The authors argue that unnecessary parts can be "easily" stripped away afterward and that operations that are required several times can be cloned by the user in advance. But neither is this stripping process of "dead code" (which is not dead, since the composition does not contain if-statements) explained in detail, nor is the drawback discussed that arises when the user must know in advance how often every operation is used; why would he then make use of automated composition techniques? Intuitively, the algorithm either considers too many or too few operations.

Apart from this conceptual flaw, the approach exhibits the same problems as the one by Srivastava [143] discussed in Sect. 3.2 even though it avoids some complexity issues due to the restriction to sequential compositions. The implementation and description of operations are not separated from each other, which imposes the same inflexibility as in the case of [143]. The composition process also relies on an SMT solver, but the fact that the solver does not need to guess statements or guards, the complexity is significantly less than in the case of [143]. The obvious consequence is that the potentially achievable programs are much simpler.

One advantage of both this approaches over most service composition approaches is that it allows for rather complex preconditions and postconditions. In general, it seems possible that it works with preconditions and postconditions that are not only conjunctions but arbitrarily structured formulas. For example, the postconditions of the query consist of a conjunction of rules. In contrast, current approaches for automated service composition only allow conjunctions of ground literals.[1]

To summarize, there are relevant recent approaches to program synthesis that exhibit both a significant intersection and significant differences with automated service composition. The most important commonalities are the goal to automatically synthesize software and that this is done on the basis of implicit goal descriptions and with a library of components described through preconditions and postconditions (of unequal complexity). The most important differences are that program synthesis approaches do not distinguish between the implementation and the description of operations, which reduces these approaches to work with very simple operations, mostly numeric or set theoretic ones. Certainly, the fields can learn a lot from each

---

[1]One exception is [59] where there may several initial states. Also, most approaches interpret the output variables of the request as (implicitly) existentially quantified.

other, and it would be interesting to combine them in the long term view in order to unify the power of both domain theories and interface-based composition.

4.3.2.2 Information Integration

In 2002, an approach related to information integration was proposed by Ponnekanti and Fox [124]. The basis of the approach is an entity structure like an entity relationship model. A query sent to the composition algorithm consists of the entities involved, provided attributes of these entities, constraints on the entities, and the requested attributes or relations for the entities. For example, a query may ask for a composition that works on two objects X and Y of the type *Person*, for both of which the first name and the last name are given as inputs, and for which we are interested in a shortest path to get from the house of X to the house of Y. That is, there is a relation *DrivingDirections*$(\cdot, \cdot)$ that we want to compute for the pair (X, Y). The controller is assumed to have a table of each attribute and each relation available, which is partially computed by the invocation of services. The data flow between services is fixed in their description that matches the names of these tables maintained by the composed algorithm.

Within its limited range, this technique is substantially better than many of the propositional logical approaches discussed above that ignore the data flow. The advantage is that the communication with services always happens with respect to particular objects, and it is also possible to request the same attribute for two different objects of the same type; in the propositional logic systems, this query type does not make sense. Of course, there are some limitations. For example, one can determine the price of a product as the attribute of the respective product entity, but the price cannot be converted into a different currency. The reason is that the predicates are only defined over entities but not over attributes, and a particular piece of information can only be either an entity or an attribute. Apart from this limitation, the approach is fairly easy to understand and seems to have the potential of reasonable usage in practice.

4.3.2.3 PDDL-Based Approaches

Initial Model

Joachim Peer proposed a technique that composes constant-based service invocations [119]. The algorithm receives a set of services with preconditions and postconditions and a goal specification. As an example, he proposes a goal that requires the composition to "send the name of the city with ZIP code 30313 to the email address john@some.com". Services can be information gathering, e.g., a service that computes the state and the city given a ZIP code, and world-altering services, e.g., a service that sends an email. The composition algorithm consists of two parts. First, a simplified problem is reduced in which constraints on concrete values are ignored.

Then, the information-gathering services of the plan are invoked in order to extend the knowledge about the world. Second, the gathered knowledge is added to the initial situation s_0, and the problem is solved again. The composition problem is encoded in the planning language PDDL, so that it can be solved with any standard planner. The objects encoded in the PDDL problem are constants referring to objects in the real world. Since the objects do refer to concrete data items instead of generic data objects (what would be called a variable in a programming language), the algorithm does not create a composition with a data flow between service operations. This is the same as programming a sequence of function calls where every argument passed to a function call is a *constant* and not an output of previous function calls. These constants are either given initially or obtained through the first phase of the algorithm.

In the presented form, the approach exhibits two major flaws. First, it simply merges input and outputs to the general concept of *parameters* in PDDL. The conceptual problem is that we cannot encode information-gathering service operations in classical PDDL, because then an invocation is not possible unless we already know the desired information, which is simply a normal parameters such as the inputs, in advance. A more detailed discussion of this problem was published earlier by McDermott [97], which is even cited by Peer; however, this issue was simply ignored. Second, the actually interesting part of the algorithm, which is the first phase, is not described. The second phase is simple and could be also considered as a simple Prolog query. The world-altering services, which have no outputs, are encoded as rules, and the knowledge initially given or gathered in the first phase are assertions. But the interesting question is obviously the first phase of the algorithm, in which it is determined for which predicates a partial grounding is desired and queried. Given the fact that this first phase would be the actual contribution, but that it is not discussed at all, the approach does not exceed a preliminary conceptual level.

Extended Models

Klusch et al. propose a PDDL encoding that avoids these problems [71, 72]. The idea is to introduce a special predicate *agentHasKnowledgeAbout*(x) to assert that the object x is available. For each input of a service operation, the predicate is part of its precondition, and for each output, it is part of the postconditions. Having this meta predicate at hand, the planner can only use data objects as inputs that have been made available either in the request or by previous service calls. The approach is based on both HTN planning and classical planning. It first tries to find a solution using a simplified form of HTN planning, and, if no solution can be found that way, it applies a classical planner.

In spite of the generally good idea, there are quite some problems with their approach. First, the overall explanation of the approach is unduly superficial. For example, HTN planning and classical planning are quite distinct approaches, but they simply mix the two without a detailed explanation of how this is done. Second, there are several conceptual flaws with respect to the planning problem definition. For example, the paper uses real world entities in the planning problem, e.g., the patient *Mikka*. But this does not make sense in combination with the *agentHasKnowledge-About* predicate, because either we know that Mikka exists (then we can use it) or we do not (then we cannot even model this object). The problem is that the semantics of the *agentHasKnowledgeAbout* predicate is that it asserts whether or not a *data container* (in programming languages we would call it a variable) has a value assigned or not; hence, it implements the check $x \neq undefined$. However, this semantics does not make sense when applied to real entities. Third, the resulting encoding into PDDL suggests that it can be solved with standard planners, but it effectively cannot due to complexity issues. The reason is that the set of objects in the PDDL problem is the set of data containers that is used to pass information among the service operations, and we do not know in advance how many such containers are necessary. Even for relatively small sizes, e.g., 30, the resulting planning problem cannot be solved even with highly advanced planning tools.[2] In their implementation, they only use one or at most two variables *per type*, which is equal to the assumption that we already know in advance what data we will need; but then, data flow planning is obsolete. Summarizing, the approach brings a small conceptual improvement, but its overall quality is rather weak.

A third approach that is based on a PDDL encoding was proposed by Vuković et al. [157]. The core idea is pretty similar to those of Peer and Klusch et al. The main difference is that no particular predicate for the availability of data is used, such as the *agentHasKnowledgeAbout* predicate in [72]; this makes one wonder how it is avoided that undefined variables are used. The approach lacks from the same complexity problem as Klusch et al. does, even though their evaluation suggests that the approach is efficient. Since none of the earlier approaches [72, 97, 119] is discussed, I cannot identify a particular novelty of the approach.

4.3.2.4 Limitation by Requiring Full Precondition Coverage

Another approach-based based on simple first-order logical preconditions and postconditions was proposed by Bartalos and Bieliková [14, 16]. In this approach, a service is described by ontologically typed inputs and outputs and by so-called *conditions*. A condition is a formula that contains symbols for predicates, conjunction, disjunction, and negation; so no function symbols or quantifiers are allowed. A composition is a DAG where every node is a service invocation and a link between service s_1 and s_2 exists only if the postcondition of s_1 implies the precondition of s_2. The paper defines the logical implication in an optimistic way, such that condition c_2 is said to be implied by condition c_1 if there is one clause in the disjunctive normal form (DNF) of c_1 that implies at least one clause of the DNF of c_2. A composition is a solution for the request, if, for each desired output, there is one service that provides it. In addition to the explicit conditions, the approach also considers ontological matchmaking in the data flow; outputs can be used whenever they are more specific than what was requested.

The strong restrictions used in the definition of a composition help create a highly efficient composition algorithm but are equally highly limiting. On one hand, the

---

[2]I used the FastDownward algorithm to verify this claim.

requirement that a service covers the *complete* preconditions of its successor in a composition allows for a preprocessing step in which all possible ways to chain two services can be computed. This allows to answer queries in fractions of seconds. On the other hand, the set of possible compositions is extremely reduced by this assumption, because preconditions of services cannot be composed from two independent operations. For example, consider that we want to use a service that sends some information to all reliable clients that have completed an order in the last month, and suppose that there are two services that compute from a given set of clients all those that are reliable or completed a purchase in the last month respectively. A valid composition invokes one of them with the input set and then the other with the result of the first operation; the result can then be passed to the third processing service. However, this is not possible here, because the preconditions of the third service cannot be satisfied by any of the former two alone. Another issue is that the simplified treatment of disjunctive conditions cannot be considered sound. Summarizing, the approach allows to consider a significant extent of semantics in the service descriptions. An efficient composition of these services is enabled by a simplified evaluation of the conditions and by a rigorous restriction on possible compositions.

4.3.3 I/O-Relational Approaches for Infinite Spaces

Approaches belonging to this subclass consider the possibility of producing arbitrary new information by the application of operations. The invocation of an operation produces (if it has any outputs) a new datum, which can possibly be used as inputs for other operations. The set of possible compositions is infinite, because we can potentially create ever new pieces of information.

4.3.3.1 Term-Algebraic Program Synthesis

The first solutions for automated software composition at all were proposed by Manna and Waldinger [93, 94]. Their approach is based on an algebraic *term transformation system*. The request consists of a precondition and a goal term that shall be computed. The basis for the composition process are transformation rules that assert admissible ways to rewrite terms. For example, an transformation rule $v \cdot 0 \Rightarrow 0$ asserts that one can renounce a factor multiplied with 0. Based on the resolution calculus, they propose a method that allows to rewrite the initially desired goal term into other goals until the trivial goal *true* is reached. The program is obtained by the term unifications used to apply the transformation rules.

The main difference between this type of automatic programming and service composition is that operations are described in terms of other operations. The semantics of an operation in deductive synthesis is encoded in transformation rules. The left-hand side of the rule states the invocation of an operation and the right-hand side states what we know about the result of the invocation; that is, how we can replace the invocation. For example, the rule $reverse(u) \Rightarrow reverse(tail(u)) <> [head(u)]$ defines the postcondition of inverting a nonempty list u. So the semantics of *reverse* is expressed in terms of itself (recursion) and other operations *tail* and *head*. Rules may also be bound to some condition, which we would call precondition. In a way, the transformation rules have similarities with methods in HTN planning (discussed in Sect. 3.3), because they describe how a term (possibly a complex service) can be rewritten.

When discussing their approach, it is important to distinguish the underlying algebraic calculus from the way how they apply it. My assertion is that the way how they encode composition problems and how they perform deductive synthesis is apparently different from the way how composition problems are encoded today. However, I do not want to give the impression that the algebraic calculus used by Manna and Waldinger is unsuitable for service composition in general. In contrast, it seems that the term transformation system is so general that it could also be used to encode the type of service composition we are using in the planning context nowadays. Still, we can only discuss an approach to the extent to which the calculus is explicitly used for the particular problem; otherwise we could also argue that Turing presented a mechanism that can be used for service composition by proposing a model of computation.

The most crucial problem with deductive program synthesis for today's research is that we are left with the lack of evaluation. Except the very vague explanations in [114], there is virtually no information about the runtime performance of their algorithm on the machines that were recent in the respective time and much less of how those algorithm would perform today. Of course, complexity issues cannot be resolved with (polynomially) faster computations, but at least it would be easier to compare the approaches. Unless somebody reanimates this algebraic approach, deductive program synthesis stands behind service composition like a shadow of which it is unclear how it relates to the currently developed techniques.

Summarizing, while deductive synthesis in the presented form is hardly compatible with a modern view on software development, we can still learn a lot from this early attempt. Of course, the encoding chosen in [93, 94] exhibits a connection between description and implementation that can be hardly considered timely. On the other hand, current composition approaches completely lack built-in operations for basic data structures. It would be advantageous to compose not only business service operations but also set operations such as *head*. Together with the knowledge $y = head(x) \wedge sortedBy(x, price) \Rightarrow cheapestOf(y, x)$, the composition algorithm could be enhanced with very useful theories that help treat different data structures or basic arithmetical operations. Hence, we should rather seek to complement the modern approaches with the early stage attempts.

4.3.3.2 PDDL-Modification

In one of the first approaches so automated service composition, Drew McDermott extended the PDDL specification in order to make it suitable for service composition

[97]. McDermott realized that PDDL lacks the possibility to specify the creation of new information; so he added the notion of step-values, which are like the (single) output of an action. The output values have a type and may or may not have a default value. If an output has a default value and if another service is used whose precondition make assertions about that value, the planner inserts a special predicate *verify* that signals that, in case that a solution is found, a case distinction must be inserted. In an initial run, the algorithm assumes that the verify-predicates are all true. If a solution is found, the algorithm is restarted with the initial situation being the first situation in which a verify-predicate occurs, modified in a way that the statement to be verified is negated. Starting from there, the algorithm tries to find a solution for the alternative branch. In this way, the algorithm is able to compose programs with conditional branches.

Even though the approach does not exhibit particular shortcomings, it has never been adopted or served as a basis to build upon by later approaches. I already discussed some approaches based on PDDL that do not make use of McDermott's modifications. One problem could be that the supposed advantage of PDDL is that it serves as an input for standard planners but that a significant part of the specification is not covered by any planner; this becomes obviously even worse with the additional extension made in [97]. At time of writing, at least the planner Optop written by McDermott himself is available at his website. Bertoli et al. claim that the approach cannot cope with protocol specifications [23], but given the fact that protocols can be encoded simply through propositional assertions in the preconditions and postconditions of services, this claim cannot be justified.

I think that there are three arguments why Optop is not the end of the story for service composition. First, we have seen that nonfunctional properties are an important aspect of service composition, but these are not considered at all. Since there is no straight-forward way in PDDL to consider these properties, another extension of PDDL would be required. Second, a lot of research related to service composition is concerned not only to how to *model* the composition problem but also of how the space of possible compositions is *traversed*. McDermott proposes a search based on a regression-match graph, but there are many other possibilities about how the search space can be traversed. Third, the paper reflects only a preliminary stage of research without any evaluation. We have no information of how the approach performs in comparison to others; the goal and the achievements of the paper is only to give a proof of concept that estimated regression works for service composition. Also, it does not provide for loops, which are inevitable for most applications. Hence, we have seen a sound but rudimentary solution for automated service composition, and there is plenty space for improvements.

4.3.3.3 General Unbounded Search

In our recent works, we have proposed a technique to search for service compositions without a limitation of the number of variables [109]. The input of the composition algorithm is precondition and postcondition as conjunctions of literals, a set of services described in the same way, and a vector of bounds for the nonfunctional properties. The algorithm searches backwards starting from the desired postconditions and builds a composition by *prepending* an operation invocation to the current composition in each step. Hence, compositions computed by this approach are only *sequences* of operation invocations. A service operation is a candidate for being prepended if its postcondition contains at least one literal that is required for the precondition of the currently considered composition. During the composition process, the algorithm may introduce an arbitrary number of new variables (as yet undefined sources of some of the inputs of prepended operation invocations). Every (partial) composition is associated with a vector of nonfunctional properties, which are assumed to increase or decrease monotonically. The algorithm returns a *stream* of Pareto optimal compositions.

The algorithm can also insert more complex control structures if these are hidden in building blocks derived from domain independent templates [107, 108]. These templates are more specific with respect to the control flow elements than the ones used by Srivastava et al. in [143], e.g., the rough code within a loop body is already set. This structural restriction increases the feasibility of the approach, because otherwise there would be too many candidate implementations. The templates contain placeholders for boolean expressions (usually of if-statements), service invocations, and auxiliary predicates. For example, a template FILTER takes a set A as input and computes the subset of elements that satisfy a particular property. For every $a \in A$, a (still undetermined) service s is invoked and determines the value of some (still undetermined) property of a. The obtained value is tested against some (still undetermined) condition. The item a is added to the output set A' if this test has a positive result. This template can then be used to, say, filter a set of books by those that are available. In [108], we present a template instantiation technique that can be directly integrated with the composition algorithm described above. Similar to the approach of Srivastava et al. template here are a *possible guide* to find a solution but they do not encode the actual behavior of the composition.

The formal model underlying our approach is almost the same as the one of Hoffmann et al. [59] with the crucial difference that we do not assume strict forward effects. That is, we allow the postconditions of services and the postconditions specified in the query to related outputs to the inputs. On one hand, this difference has a significant computantional impact in that it precludes the possibility to ground the problem to a (finite) propositional model. In fact, the composition problem probably becomes undecidable by this assumption. On the other hand, it allows to specify much richer requirement definitions that are much closer to the intuition of a specification of actual behavior than lose properties of the ingoing and outgoing data. While undecidability is certainly not a desirable theoretical feature, for practical applications of service composition undecidability is not much worse than highly exponential complexities. That is, it does not matter whether the algorithm runs forever or whether it terminates after some weeks or even years saying that no answer exists; either it finds a solution fast or we must implement the desired component by ourselves. So, independently from decidability questions, the goal must be to find solutions fast if they exist; proving that no solution exists is of minor practical importance.

The main drawback of the approach is that it does not support diverging control flow branches. That is, if-statements are only allowed in templates and only if the template postconditions are still deterministic (purely conjunctive); that is, the composition algorithm does not need to plan two or more possible program states in parallel. McDermott resolved this problem by first planning optimistically and then planning the alternative branches afterward. However, the current version of our composition algorithm does not provide this clearly desirable functionality. Hence, the treatment of alternative and diverging control flow branches remains important and, given a backward search, nontrivial future work.

Summarizing, our approach provides an alternative to the model proposed by McDermott that considers nonfunctional properties and complex predefined control structures but that still lacks the ability to compose diverging control flows. Instead of investigating the problem on a language-specific level like PDDL, we prefer an independent mathematical model that defines a search space that can then be traversed by search algorithms such as A^*.

4.3.4 Concluding Discussion

The techniques discussed in Sect. 4.3.1 provide good formal models and interesting ideas, but the lack of relations between inputs and outputs of operations hinders semantically meaningful composition. The more detailed description of inputs and outputs based on first-order logical formulas is an improvement over the approaches discussed in Sects. 4.1 and 4.2, but meaningful composition requires to relate inputs to outputs, which is not the case in these systems. Still, at least for the system proposed by Hoffmann et al. [59, 60], the model has a native support for meaningful composition if the assumption of strict forward effects is dropped. On the other hand, dropping this assumption probably renders the task unsolvable with current planning algorithms, so practically solving the problem without strict forward effects certainly entails quite some work. Another issue of the two techniques discussed here is that they do not incorporate any notion of nonfunctional properties (Table 4.3).

Program synthesis is an interesting field but is somehow out of phase with respect to the underlying operation model. The fact that we can only use operations whose implementation corresponds to the description seems to be a strong limitation. The reader always has the impression that those techniques only work on very specific domains, e.g., numerics and sets. On the other hand, it is quite possible that these composition models can be extended such that they decouple implementation and description. The advantage of such a system would be tremendous because it would allow for operation descriptions with both uninterpreted and interpreted predicates. However, this integration is currently not visible.

The remaining approaches address what I would call the core of automated service composition. The user can specify a desired behavior of the composition in terms of uninterpreted predicates that relate the requested outputs to the provided inputs. Unfortunately, the approaches described by Peer [119], Klusch et al. [72],

Table 4.3 Overview of approaches without a given structure that rely on first-order logic descriptions

Name	TH	QoS	Alt	Loops	Particular Strengths	Particular Weaknesses
Ambite et al.	●	○	○	○	good formalism, structured data	no description of composition queries
Hoffmann et al.	●	○	○	○	great formalism, extendible unbound search	no relation between inputs and outputs
Gulwani et al.	○	○	○	○	good performance, complex postconditions	implem.=descr., permutated operations
Ponnekanti et al.	○	○	○	○	simple algorithm	very limited composition possibilities
Peer	●	○	○	○		outputs are ordinary PDDL parameters
Klusch et al.	●	○	○	○		poor performance through grounding
Vuković et al.	●	○	○	○		no discussion of related work, no novelty
Bartalos et al.	●	○	○	○		
Manna et al.	○	○	●	●	good formalism, recursion	no QoS, no evaluation
McDermott	●	○	●	○	unbounded model, alternative branches	not further elaborated
Mohr et al.	●	●	●	●	unbounded model, QoS considered, basic loops	no native support for alternatives

TH = Hierarchical Type System, *QoS* = Quality of Service (NF-Properties), *Alt* = Compositions with alternative control flows (if-statements), *Loops* = Compositions with loops

● fully supported ○ not supported. The order in which the approaches were discussed. The *double lines* separate the approaches discussed in different subsections from each other. Literature references can be found in the respective discussions of the approaches

and Vuković [157] exhibit significant formal flaws or are not sufficiently elaborated to actually apply them. Also, nonfunctional aspects play virtually no role. The technique presented by Ponnekanti and Fox [124] is well elaborated and appears quite useful. Probably the only concern against their technique is that the set of possible queries is very limited, because we can only ask for attributes of entities. Among all approaches discussed so far, McDermott [97] and our own work [106] are the only solutions to the composition problem that do not exhibit any of these limitations.

However, even the composition algorithms discussed in [97, 109] can only be considered initial steps. One problem is that none of the two has a complete support for all of the functional and nonfunctional aspects that would be relevant for composition. For example, McDermott does not treat nonfunctional properties or loops. Our own algorithm covers nonfunctional aspects but has only quite limited support for conditional statements and loops. In particular, the consideration of diverging control flows is not possible in a straight-forward manner.

Clearly the greatest challenge of unbounded service composition is to optimize the runtime of the search process *without simplifying the model*. Semantically meaningful composition may induce semi-decidability, which seems to be the case in [97, 109]. However, the strategy should not be to downgrade the problem but to enable a fast finding of solutions if they exist. In practice, the difference between, say, NEXPTIME and undecidability is almost irrelevant, because we do not need a *proof* for the nonexistence of a solution. Either we can find a solution fast or we implement it manually, but we do not care about whether no solution was returned in time because no one exists or because the algorithm was not fast enough to find it. I do not say that it is not a good idea to solve a simplified version of the model in an interior routine whose parameters are iteratively adjusted to continuously expand the search space. But we should not unnecessarily simplify the task itself only to obtain fast algorithms (that solve irrelevant problems).

Chapter 5
Conclusion and Outlook

5.1 Summary

This section briefly summarizes the state of the art of the two main classes of automated software composition and answers the research questions initially posed in Chap. 1.

5.1.1 Template-Based Approaches

Template-based service composition is currently split into three rather isolated branches. All the approaches aim at (possibly recursively) instantiating a given template under a given set of constraints.

1. There are approaches that ignore functional aspects and aim at optimally instantiating a template with respect to quality of service such as price, reliability, execution time, etc.
   Within this group, approaches can be further classified by the complexity of the control flow (simple, i.e., sequential or none at all, vs. complex) and by the output, which may be an optimal solution (IP models), an approximate solution (heuristic search or genetic programming), or several Pareto optimal solutions.
2. There are approaches that consider constraints related to functional properties that affect the admissibility of instantiations.
   Within this group, approaches focus either on discovery aspects (finding appropriate operations for placeholders based on IOPE specifications or task names), dependencies (maintain a correct order of invocation of operations of used services, observe conflicts among services, or guarantee transactional properties), and problem domain specific requirements (such as maximum hotel costs, traveling time, etc.).
3. Some few approaches consider a (recursive) refinement of templates in which the placeholders are not replaced by atomic service operations but entire subroutines.
   Within this subclass, we distinguish approaches that instantiate placeholders nonrecursively (a nonrecursive routine computes the composition that fits into the placeholder) or recursively (placeholders are replaced by atomic operations or

© The Author(s) 2016
F. Mohr, *Automated Software and Service Composition*,
SpringerBriefs in Computer Science, DOI 10.1007/978-3-319-34168-2_5

recursively by instantiating another template that implements the respective place-holder).

Surprisingly, there are only very few approaches that consider aspects that belong into more than one of the subclasses. In general, we can think of a composition system that considers *all* of the aspects presented in the papers in this class, because they are generally complementary. However, only some works can be considered to look at more than one of these aspects. For example, [38, 50] consider quality of service besides the main focus of their work (transactional properties, hierarchical instanti-ation, etc.). Probably, even though being one of the first systems of all, METEOR-S considers functional discovery, QoS, and domain specific constraints and can hence be considered the most complete one [3].

5.1.2   Approaches Without a Given Structure

Service composition that does not rely on a given template aims at converting declar-ative requirement definitions into imperative implementations. The requirement def-initions are (at least indirectly) given in form of logical preconditions and postcon-ditions, which constitute a planning problem.

In general, the behavior of an operation can be described either through propo-sitional logic or through first-order logic. On one hand, most approaches are based on propositionally described preconditions and postconditions, which reduces to a set theoretic planning problem. Even though some of them are more complex due to dependencies among the operations (e.g., in the ASTRO project), most of the addressed problems can be solved in polynomial time. On the other hand, there are some approaches that allow for limited predicate logical descriptions of the behavior of operations. Usually, these still forbid uninterpreted function symbols, and quanti-fier usage is also limited. However, they are more expressive because they can work on properties defined between inputs and outputs of an operation.

5.1.3   Answers to the Initial Research Questions

To summarize the results of this work, I answer the three questions posed in the introduction.

1. *Which types of automated software composition problems exist?*
   There are two very general types of automated software composition problems, which can be distinguished by the question whether or not a structure that describes the behavior of the desired software artifact is given. Template-based composition may consider both functional and nonfunctional aspects, but most current approaches are highly specialized in only one of the two. Composition

based on implicit descriptions may be based on propositional or first-order logic. Figure 5.1 shows the more specific subclasses identified in this book.

2. *Which are the typical use cases where these problems occur?*
   The typical use case of template-based composition is that a workflow must be refined in the presence of a concrete composition input or user specific preferences or constraints. The client of the system is somebody from the domain rather than a software developer. The typical use case of composition based on implicit behavior descriptions is that we want to enhance an imperative or functional development environment by the possibility to declaratively state conditions on variables such that the concrete implementation that satisfies these conditions is automatically determined by the environment. The client of the system is a software developer.

3. *Which are the most prominent solution paradigms for the different types?*
   Composition based on explicit behavior descriptions is done mainly through integer programming, heuristic search, and genetic programming. In the case of recursive refinements, hierarchical AI planning methods such as HTN planning are used. Composition based on implicit behavior descriptions is done either through the notion of AI planning, algebraic term replacement systems, and theorem proving.

5.2 Discussion

The large number of publications in the field shows not only a broad interest in automated software composition but also the variety of aspects that are relevant for the problem. Many of the approaches presented here were published on venues like the Conference on Services Computing (SCC), the International Conference on Web Services (ICWS), or the International Conference on Service Oriented Computing (ICSOC). The mere existence of these (quite large) venues shows that many people are interested in the topic. At the same time, the wide range of approaches shows that automated composition is interesting from many different viewpoints.

However, looking at the development of automated composition during the last decade, we should be aware of an alarming trend. Automated composition had a great upturn in the five years from 2002 to 2006, but this momentum became to dwindle in 2012. My explanation for this development is that, at the beginning of the century, practitioners recognized (again) that automation in software development has a great potential. But the little convincing research results (from the practical viewpoint) made the interest vanish again. This reminds of the development of AI in the last century.

I think that there are basically two reasons for this situation.

- *Wrong things are done.*
  Apparently, many authors think that the hype on services is (was) a self-sufficient evidence for the relevance of automated composition. It is not! Many people doubt

Fig. 5.1 Classification system for software composition based on existing approaches

in the potential of automated programming, and, given the background of almost 40 years without success seems to give them right. This will not stop until automated composition will have become a part of everyday programming.

This fact is, however, frequently ignored. Instead of working towards a reality with automated composition, many papers show striking evaluation results achieved on unreasonably trivial problems that will never ever be part of a relevant composition setting. I would highly prefer a treatment of relevant and hard problems with mediocre results, (which can be improved) over the treatment of irrelevant and trivial problems with great results, (which few people care about).[1]

People outside the community first ask *for what* the technology can be used, and *then* (perhaps) whether the algorithm finds solution within a second. Hence, the goal should be to make the scenario of software composition more *credible* and *applicable* and not to generate ever better algorithms on uninteresting subproblems.

- *Things are done in the wrong manner.*

Writing this book, I became aware that many authors do not know at all the field they publish in. The incredible number of outsorted papers shows that many authors do not even know the most important related work. But also in many approaches presented in this book, the discussion of related papers appears to fulfill only an alibi function. Quite often, it seems that the authors did not carefully read or understand the papers they cite; in particular the related papers are only described highly superficially but the *differences* between the own and the related approach often are not discussed. Hopefully, this book helps reduce the obstacle to study (and know) related work.

Another problem is that many authors do not recognize or do not care about obvious conceptual flaws in their publications. Many approaches are too abstract and model-oriented, and the formalisms are often heavily flawed. Correctness or executability of the resulting compositions does not seem to be a relevant issue. There is nothing wrong with a formal and abstract model, but it must be clear that the assumptions that the compositions obtained from the model can be translated into working compositions.

The problem is that this type of research hinders progress. If I am not aware of the other or if the other only provides heavily flawed contributions, I must begin from scratch. This is a tremendous waste of human resources.

Is everything bad? No! This book presents a lot of papers with great ideas and approaches on automated software composition. Building systematically on top of these with high quality contributions should allow us to see automated composition become reality—or to see that nobody wants to use it. In any case, much high quality work is necessary to let this vision become true.

---

[1] One of my papers was rejected at IJCAI with the comment that the addressed problem is undecidable and, hence, not relevant. What a conclusion! If decidability is the criterion for relevance, why do FOL solvers exist and are used?

5.3 Outlook

Once again, the most important issue is to give evidence for the actual necessity of this type of composition, i.e., that software composition is not a phantom problem. Many papers are motivated by the "enormous and ever-growing number of services", but those legions of services seem to be hidden quite effectively from potential customers in the real world. Automated software composition faces the objection of solving a theoretic problem that will never occur in practice, e.g., because semantic descriptions do not exist. The setting assumed for automated composition will not come into existence without a strong incentive, and this incentive can only be the existence of high quality tools that provide a better net utility for developers than nonautomated systems.

I see different research prospects for the two main classes of composition presented in the book. In template-based composition, a unified composition model that brings together the achievements of all the existing approaches should be the goal. That is, service usage constraints, hierarchical instantiation, QoS optimization, business constraints, etc., should be considered simultaneously and not in isolation. As a basis, one may suggest [3, 38, 50] and established models such as [20, 136]. Future work in the area of composition without templates is to provide feasibility for composition with expressive description languages (FOL). The works of Hoffmann et al. [60] (without limitation of strict forward effect), McDermott [97], and my own ones [106, 109] provide closely related formal problem descriptions that can be used to build on top. An interesting other aspect is the integration of nondeterminism as covered by Bertoli et al. [23].

For both cases, the integration of user interaction for choosing the desired (among several Pareto optimal, possibly relaxed) solutions would complement the model with respect to the client necessities.

References

1. Agarwal, V., Chafle, G., Dasgupta, K., Karnik, N., Kumar, A., Mittal, S.: Synthy: a system for end to end composition of web services. Web Semant.: Sci., Serv. Agents World Wide Web **3**(4), 311–339 (2005)
2. Agarwal, V., Dasgupta, K., Karnik, N., Kumar, A., Kundu, A., Mittal, S., Srivastava, B.: A service creation environment based on end to end composition of web services. In: Proceedings of the 14th International Conference on World Wide Web, pp. 128–137. ACM (2005)
3. Aggarwal, R., Verma, K., Miller, J., Milnor, W.: Constraint driven web service composition in METEOR-S. In: Proceedings of the IEEE International Conference on Services Computing (SCC), pp. 23–30 (2004)
4. Ai, L., Tang, M.: Qos-based web service composition accommodating inter-service dependencies using minimal-conflict hill-climbing repair genetic algorithm. In: IEEE Fourth International Conference on eScience, pp. 119–126. IEEE (2008)
5. Akkiraju, R., Srivastava, B., Ivan, A.A., Goodwin, R., Syeda-Mahmood, T.: Semaplan: combining planning with semantic matching to achieve web service composition. In: International Conference on Web Services (ICWS), pp. 37–44. IEEE (2006)
6. Alrifai, M., Risse, T.: Combining global optimization with local selection for efficient qos-aware service composition. In: Proceedings of the 18th International Conference on World Wide Web, pp. 881–890. ACM (2009)
7. Alrifai, M., Skoutas, D., Risse, T.: Selecting skyline services for qos-based web service composition. In: Proceedings of the 19th International Conference on World Wide Web, pp. 11–20. ACM (2010)
8. Ambite, J.L., Kapoor, D.: Automatically Composing Data Workflows With Relational Descriptions and Shim Services. Springer, Berlin (2007)
9. Ardagna, D., Pernici, B.: Adaptive service composition in flexible processes. IEEE Trans. Softw. Eng. **33**(6), 369–384 (2007)
10. Arpinar, I.B., Zhang, R., Aleman-Meza, B., Maduko, A.: Ontology-driven web services composition platform. Inf. Syst. E-Bus. Manag. **3**(2), 175–199 (2005)
11. Aversano, L., Canfora, G., Ciampi, A.: An algorithm for web service discovery through their composition. In: Proceedings of IEEE International Conference on Web Services, pp. 332–339 (2004)
12. Aydın, O., Cicekli, N.K., Cicekli, I.: Automated web services composition with the event calculus. In: Engineering Societies in the Agents World VIII, pp. 142–157. Springer (2008)
13. Barakat, L., Miles, S., Poernomo, I., Luck, M.: Efficient multi-granularity service composition. In: Proceedings of the IEEE International Conference on Web Services, pp. 227–234 (2011)
14. Bartalos, P., Bieliková, M.: Fast and scalable semantic web service composition approach considering complex pre/postconditions. In: Proceedings of the 2009 Congress on Services, pp. 414–421. IEEE (2009)

© The Author(s) 2016
F. Mohr, *Automated Software and Service Composition*,
SpringerBriefs in Computer Science, DOI 10.1007/978-3-319-34168-2

15. Bartalos, P., Bieliková, M.: Semantic web service composition framework based on parallel processing. In: Proceedings of the Conference on Commerce and Enterprise Computing, pp. 495–498. IEEE (2009)

16. Bartalos, P., Bieliková, M.: QoS aware semantic web service composition approach considering pre/postconditions. In: Proceedings of the International Conference on Web Services, pp. 345–352. IEEE (2010)

17. ter Beek, M., Moruzzi, V.G.: Web service composition approaches: from industrial standards to formal methods. In: Proceedings of the Second International Conference on Internet and Web Applications and Services. IEEE (2007)

18. Benatallah, B., Perrin, O., Rabhi, F.A., Godart, C.: Web service computing: overview and directions. In: Handbook of Nature-Inspired and Innovative Computing, pp. 553–574. Springer, Heidelberg (2006)

19. Berardi, D., Calvanese, D., De Giacomo, G., Hull, R., Mecella, M.: Automatic composition of transition-based semantic web services with messaging. In: Proceedings of the 31st International Conference on Very large data bases, pp. 613–624. VLDB Endowment (2005)

20. Berardi, D., Calvanese, D., De Giacomo, G., Lenzerini, M., Mecella, M.: Automatic composition of e-services that export their behavior. In: Proceedings of the International Conference on Service-Oriented Computing, pp. 43–58. Springer (2003)

21. Berardi, D., De Giacomo, G., Mecella, M., Calvanese, D.: Automatic web service composition: service-tailored vs. client-tailored approaches. AI for Service Composition, p. 63 (2006)

22. Berbner, R., Spahn, M., Repp, N., Heckmann, O., Steinmetz, R.: Heuristics for qos-aware web service composition. In: Proceedings of the International Conference on Web Services, pp. 72–82. IEEE (2006)

23. Bertoli, P., Pistore, M., Traverso, P.: Automated composition of web services via planning in asynchronous domains. Artif. Intell. **174**(3), 316–361 (2010)

24. Blake, M.B., Cummings, D.J.: Workflow composition of service level agreements. In: Proceedings of the International Conference on Services Computing, pp. 138–145. IEEE (2007)

25. Blanco, E., Cardinale, Y., Vidal, M.E., El Haddad, J., Manouvrier, M., Rukoz, M.: A transactional-qos driven approach for web service composition. In: Resource Discovery, pp. 23–42. Springer, Heidelberg (2012)

26. Blum, A.L., Furst, M.L.: Fast planning through planning graph analysis. Artif. Intell. **90**(1), 281–300 (1997)

27. Bouillet, E., Feblowitz, M., Feng, H., Liu, Z., Ranganathan, A., Riabov, A.: A folksonomy-based model of web services for discovery and automatic composition. In: Proceedings of the International Conference on Services Computing, vol. 1, pp. 389–396. IEEE (2008)

28. Bouillet, E., Feblowitz, M., Liu, Z., Ranganathan, A., Riabov, A.: A faceted requirements-driven approach to service design and composition. In: Proceedings of the International Conference on Web Services, pp. 369–376. IEEE (2008)

29. Brogi, A., Corfini, S., Popescu, R.: Composition-oriented service discovery. In: Software Composition, pp. 15–30. Springer, Heidelberg (2005)

30. Calvanese, D., De Giacomo, G., Lenzerini, M., Mecella, M., Patrizi, F.: Automatic service composition and synthesis: the roman model. IEEE Data Eng. Bull. **31**(3), 18–22 (2008)

31. Canfora, G., Di Penta, M., Esposito, R., Villani, M.L.: An approach for qos-aware service composition based on genetic algorithms. In: Proceedings of the 7th Annual Conference on Genetic and Evolutionary Computation, pp. 1069–1075. ACM (2005)

32. Canfora, G., Di Penta, M., Esposito, R., Villani, M.L.: QoS-aware replanning of composite web services. In: Proceedings of the International Conference on Web Services, pp. 121–129. IEEE (2005)

33. Cardoso, A.J.S.: Quality of service and semantic composition of workflows. Ph.D. thesis, Ph.D. Dissertation, Department of Computer Science. 2002, University of Georgia, Athens, GA, USA, 215 (2002)

34. Cardoso, J., Miller, J., Sheth, A., Arnold, J.: Quality of service for workflows and web service processes. J. Web Semant. **1**, 281–308 (2004)

35. Cardoso, J., Sheth, A.: Semantic e-workflow composition. J. Intell. Inf. Syst. **21**(3), 191–225 (2003)
36. Channa, N., Li, S., Shaikh, A.W., Fu, X.: Constraint satisfaction in dynamic web service composition. In: Proceedings of the Sixteenth International Workshop on Database and Expert Systems Applications, pp. 658–664. IEEE (2005)
37. Cheikh, F., De Giacomo, G., Mecella, M.: Automatic web services composition in trustaware communities. In: Proceedings of the 3rd ACM Workshop on Secure Web Services, pp. 43–52. ACM (2006)
38. Chen, K., Xu, J., Reiff-Marganiec, S.: Markov-htn planning approach to enhance flexibility of automatic web service composition. In: Proceedings of the International Conference on Web Services, pp. 9–16. IEEE (2009)
39. Chifu, V.R., Salomie, I., Riger, A., Radoi, V.: A graph based backward chaining method for web service composition. In: Proceedings of the 5th International Conference on Intelligent Computer Communication and Processing, pp. 237–244. IEEE (2009)
40. Claro, D.B., Albers, P., Hao, J.K.: Selecting web services for optimal composition. In: ICWS International Workshop on Semantic and Dynamic Web Processes, Orlando-USA (2005)
41. Constantinescu, I., Binder, W., Faltings, B.: Service composition with directories. In: Software Composition, pp. 163–177. Springer, Heidelberg (2006)
42. Constantinescu, I., Faltings, B., Binder, W.: Large scale, type-compatible service composition. In: Proceedings of the International Conference on Web Services, pp. 506–513. IEEE (2004)
43. Constantinescu, I., Faltings, B., Binder, W.: Type based service composition. In: Proceedings of the 13th International World Wide Web Conference on Alternate Track Papers & Posters, pp. 268–269. ACM (2004)
44. De Giacomo, G., Di Ciccio, C., Felli, P., Hu, Y., Mecella, M.: Goal-based composition of stateful services for smart homes. In: On the Move to Meaningful Internet Systems: OTM 2012, pp. 194–211. Springer, Heidelberg (2012)
45. Degeler, V., Georgievski, I., Lazovik, A., Aiello, M.: Concept mapping for faster qos-aware web service composition. In: Proceedings of the International Conference on Service-Oriented Computing and Applications, pp. 1–4. IEEE (2010)
46. D'Mello, D.A., Ananthanarayana, V., Salian, S.: A review of dynamic web service composition techniques. In: Advanced Computing, pp. 85–97. Springer, Heidelberg (2011)
47. Doshi, P., Goodwin, R., Akkiraju, R., Verma, K.: Dynamic workflow composition using markov decision processes. In: Proceedings of the International Conference on Web Services, pp. 576–582. IEEE (2004)
48. Dustdar, S., Papazoglou, M.P.: Services and service composition–an introduction (services und service komposition–eine einführung). it-Information Technology (vormals it+ ti) **50**(2/2008), 86–92 (2008)
49. Dustdar, S., Schreiner, W.: A survey on web services composition. Int. J. Web Grid Serv. **1**(1), 1–30 (2005)
50. El Haddad, J., Manouvrier, M., Rukoz, M.: Tqos: transactional and qos-aware selection algorithm for automatic web service composition. IEEE Trans. Serv. Comput. **3**(1), 73–85 (2010)
51. Gao, C., Cai, M., Chen, H.: QoS-aware service composition based on tree-coded genetic algorithm. In: Proceedings of the 31st Annual International Computer Software and Applications Conference, vol. 1, pp. 361–367. IEEE (2007)
52. Gerede, Ç.E., Hull, R., Ibarra, O.H., Su, J.: Automated composition of e-services: lookaheads. In: Proceedings of the 2nd International Conference on Service Oriented Computing, pp. 252–262. ACM (2004)
53. Gulwani, S., Jha, S., Tiwari, A., Venkatesan, R.: Synthesis of loop-free programs. In: ACM SIGPLAN Notices, pp. 62–73. ACM (2011)
54. Hashemian, S.V., Mavaddat, F.: A graph-based approach to web services composition. In: Proceedings of the Symposium on Applications and the Internet, pp. 183–189. IEEE (2005)
55. Hashemian, S.V., Mavaddat, F.: A graph-based framework for composition of stateless web services. In: Proceedings of the 4th European Conference on Web Services, pp. 75–86. IEEE (2006)

56. Hassen, R.R., Nourine, L., Toumani, F.: Protocol-based web service composition. In: Proceedings of the International Conference on Service-Oriented Computing, pp. 38–53. Springer (2008)

57. Hassine, A.B., Matsubara, S., Ishida, T.: A constraint-based approach to horizontal web service composition. In: The Semantic Web-ISWC 2006, pp. 130–143. Springer, Heidelberg (2006)

58. Hoare, C.A.R.: An axiomatic basis for computer programming. Commun. ACM **12**(10), 576–580 (1969)

59. Hoffmann, J., Bertoli, P., Helmert, M., Pistore, M.: Message-based web service composition, integrity constraints, and planning under uncertainty: a new connection. J. Artif. Intell. Res. **35**, pp. 49–117 (2009)

60. Hoffmann, J., Bertoli, P., Pistore, M.: Web service composition as planning, revisited: In between background theories and initial state uncertainty. In: Proceedings of the National Conference on Artificial Intelligence, p. 1013. Menlo Park, CA, Cambridge, MA, London, AAAI Press, MIT Press, 1999 (2007)

61. Huai, J., Deng, T., Li, X., Du, Z., Guo, H.: Autosyn: a new approach to automated synthesis of composite web services with correctness guarantee. Sci. China Ser. F: Inf. Sci. **52**(9), 1534–1549 (2009)

62. Huma, Z., Gerth, C., Engels, G., Juwig, O.: Automated service composition for on-the-fly soas. In: Service-Oriented Computing, pp. 524–532. Springer, Heidelberg (2013)

63. Jiang, W., Hu, S., Lee, D., Gong, S., Liu, Z.: Continuous query for qos-aware automatic service composition. In: Proceedings of the 2012 IEEE 19th International Conference on Web Services (ICWS), pp. 50–57. IEEE (2012)

64. Jiang, W., Zhang, C., Huang, Z., Chen, M., Hu, S., Liu, Z.: Qsynth: A tool for qos-aware automatic service composition. In: Proceedings of the International Conference on Web Services, pp. 42–49. IEEE (2010)

65. Kalasapur, S., Kumar, M., Shirazi, B.: Seamless service composition (sesco) in pervasive environments. In: Proceedings of the first ACM international workshop on Multimedia service composition, pp. 11–20. ACM (2005)

66. Karakoc, E., Kardas, K., Senkul, P.: A workflow-based web service composition system. In: Proceedings of the International Conference on Web Intelligence and Intelligent Agent Technology Workshops, pp. 113–116. IEEE (2006)

67. Karakoc, E., Senkul, P.: Composing semantic web services under constraints. Expert Syst. Appl. **36**(8), 11021–11029 (2009)

68. Klein, A., Ishikawa, F., Honiden, S.: Efficient qos-aware service composition with a probabilistic service selection policy. In: Service-Oriented Computing, pp. 182–196. Springer, Heidelberg (2010)

69. Klein, A., Ishikawa, F., Honiden, S.: Efficient heuristic approach with improved time complexity for qos-aware service composition. In: Proceedings of the International Conference on Web Services, pp. 436–443. IEEE (2011)

70. Klein, A., Ishikawa, F., Honiden, S.: Towards network-aware service composition in the cloud. In: Proceedings of the 21st International Conference on World Wide Web, pp. 959–968. ACM (2012)

71. Klusch, M., Gerber, A.: Fast composition planning of owl-s services and application. In: Proceedings of the 4th European Conference on Web Services, pp. 181–190. IEEE (2006)

72. Klusch, M., Gerber, A., Schmidt, M.: Semantic web service composition planning with OWLS-XPlan. In: Proceedings of the 1st International AAAI Fall Symposium on Agents and the Semantic Web, pp. 55–62 (2005)

73. Ko, J.M., Kim, C.O., Kwon, I.H.: Quality-of-service oriented web service composition algorithm and planning architecture. J. Syst. Softw. **81**(11), 2079–2090 (2008)

74. Kona, S., Bansal, A., Blake, M.B., Gupta, G.: Generalized semantics-based service composition. In: Proceedings of the International Conference on Web Services, pp. 219–227. IEEE (2008)

75. Kona, S., Bansal, A., Gupta, G., Hite, D.: Automatic composition of semantic web services. ICWS **7**, 150–158 (2007)

76. Koza, J.R., Rice, J.P.: Automatic programming of robots using genetic programming. AAAI **92**, 194–207 (1992)
77. Küngas, P., Matskin, M.: Semantic web service composition through a p2p-based multi-agent environment. In: Agents and Peer-to-Peer Computing, pp. 106–119. Springer, Heidelberg (2006)
78. Küster, U., König-Ries, B., Stern, M., Klein, M.: Diane: an integrated approach to automated service discovery, matchmaking and composition. In: Proceedings of International Conference on World Wide Web, pp. 1033–1042. ACM (2007)
79. Lämmermann, S.: Runtime service composition via logic-based program synthesis (2002)
80. Lautenbacher, F., Bauer, B.: A survey on workflow annotation and composition approaches. In: SBPM (2007)
81. Lécué, F.: Optimizing Qos-Aware Semantic Web Service Composition. Springer, Heidelberg (2009)
82. Lécué, F., Delteil, A.: Making the difference in semantic web service composition. In: Proceedings of the National Conference on Artificial Intelligence, pp. 1383–1388. AAAI Press, MIT Press, Menlo Park, CA, Cambridge, MA, London (2007)
83. Lécué, F., Léger, A.: A formal model for semantic web service composition. In: The Semantic Web-ISWC 2006, pp. 385–398. Springer, Heidelberg (2006)
84. Lecue, F., Mehandjiev, N.: Seeking quality of web service composition in a semantic dimension. IEEE Trans. Knowl. Data Eng. **23**(6), 942–959 (2011)
85. Liang, Z., Zou, H., Yang, F., Lin, R.: A hybrid approach for the multi-constraint web service selection problem in web service composition. J. Inf. Comput. Sci. **9**(13), 3771–3781 (2012)
86. Lin, N., Kuter, U., Hendler, J.: Web service composition via problem decomposition across multiple ontologies. In: Proceedings of the Services Congress, pp. 65–72. IEEE (2007)
87. Lin, N., Kuter, U., Sirin, E.: Web service composition with user preferences. Springer, Heidelberg (2008)
88. Liu, J., Fan, C., Gu, N.: Web services automatic composition with minimal execution price. In: Proceedings of the International Conference on Web Services, pp. 302–309. IEEE (2005)
89. Ludwig, S., et al.: Single-objective versus multi-objective genetic algorithms for workflow composition based on service level agreements. In: Proceedings of the International Conference on Service-Oriented Computing and Applications, pp. 1–8. IEEE (2011)
90. Luo, Y.s., Qi, Y., Shen, L.f., Hou, D., Sapa, C., Chen, Y.: An improved heuristic for qos-aware service composition framework. In: Proceedings of the International Conference on High Performance Computing and Communications, pp. 360–367. IEEE (2008)
91. Ma, Y., Chen, L., Hui, J., Wu, J.: Cbbcm: Clustering based automatic service composition. In: Proceedings of the International Conference on Services Computing, pp. 354–361. IEEE (2011)
92. Mabrouk, N.B., Beauche, S., Kuznetsova, E., Georgantas, N., Issarny, V.: Qos-aware service composition in dynamic service oriented environments. In: Middleware 2009, pp. 123–142. Springer, Heidelberg (2009)
93. Manna, Z., Waldinger, R.: Synthesis: Dreams—programs. IEEE Trans. Softw. Eng. **SE-5**(4), 294–328 (1979)
94. Manna, Z., Waldinger, R.: A deductive approach to program synthesis. ACM Trans. Program. Lang. Syst. **2**(1), 90–121 (1980)
95. Matskin, M., Rao, J.: Value-added web services composition using automatic program synthesis. In: Web Services, E-Business, and the Semantic Web, pp. 213–224. Springer, Heidelberg (2002)
96. Maurice, A.B., Gnesi, S.: A survey on service composition approaches: from industrial standards to formal methods. In: Proceedings of the International Conference on Internet and Web Applications and Services, pp. 10–129 (2006)
97. McDermott, D.V.: Estimated-regression planning for interactions with web services. AIPS **2**, 204–211 (2002)
98. McIlraith, S., Son, T.C.: Adapting golog for composition of semantic web services. KR **2**, 482–493 (2002)

99. Medjahed, B., Bouguettaya, A., Elmagarmid, A.K.: Composing web services on the semantic web. The VLDB J. Int. J. Very Large Data Bases **12**(4), 333–351 (2003)
100. Mehandjiev, N., Lecue, F., Wajid, U., Namoun, A.: Assisted service composition for end users. In: Proceedings of the European Conference on Web Services, pp. 131–138. IEEE (2010)
101. Milanovic, N., Malek, M.: Current solutions for web service composition. IEEE Internet Comput. **8**(6), 51–59 (2004)
102. Mitra, S., Basu, S., Kumar, R.: Local and on-the-fly choreography-based web service composition. In: Proceedings of the International Conference on Web Intelligence, pp. 521–527. IEEE (2007)
103. Mitra, S., Kumar, R., Basu, S.: Automated choreographer synthesis for web services composition using i/o automata. In: IEEE International Conference on Web Services, 2007 (ICWS 2007), pp. 364–371. IEEE (2007)
104. Mitra, S., Kumar, R., Basu, S.: Optimum decentralized choreography for web services composition. In: Proceedings of the International Conference on Services Computing, vol. 2, pp. 395–402. IEEE (2008)
105. Mohr, F.: Issues of automated software composition in ai planning. In: Proceedings of the 29th International Conference on Automated Software Engineering, pp. 895–898. ACM (2014)
106. Mohr, F., Jungmann, A., Buning, H.K.: Automated online service composition. In: Proceedings of the International Conference on Services Computing, pp. 57–64. IEEE (2015)
107. Mohr, F., Kleine Büning, H.: Semi-automated software composition through generated components. In: Proceedings of International Conference on Information Integration and Web-based Applications and Services, p. 676. ACM (2013)
108. Mohr, F., Walther, S.: Template-based generation of semantic services. In: Software Reuse for Dynamic Systems in the Cloud and Beyond, pp. 188–203. Springer, Heidelberg (2014)
109. Mohr, F., Walther, S.: Template-based generation of semantic services. In: Journal of Systems and Software. Springer, Heidelberg (2015)
110. Mokhtar, S.B., Fournier, D., Georgantas, N., Issarny, V.: Context-aware service composition in pervasive computing environments. In: Rapid Integration of Software Engineering Techniques, pp. 129–144. Springer, Heidelberg (2006)
111. Mokhtar, S.B., Liu, J., Georgantas, N., Issarny, V.: Qos-aware dynamic service composition in ambient intelligence environments. In: Proceedings of the 20th IEEE/ACM International Conference on Automated Software Engineering, pp. 317–320. ACM (2005)
112. Montagut, F., Molva, R., Golega, S.T.: Automating the composition of transactional web services. J. Web Serv. Res. **5**(1), 24 (2008)
113. Narayanan, S., McIlraith, S.A.: Simulation, verification and automated composition of web services. In: Proceedings of the 11th International Conference on World Wide Web, pp. 77–88. ACM (2002)
114. Oh, S.C., Lee, D., Kumara, S.R.: A comparative illustration of ai planning-based web services composition. ACM SIGecom Exch. **5**(5), 1–10 (2005)
115. Okutan, C., Cicekli, N.K.: A monolithic approach to automated composition of semantic web services with the event calculus. Knowl.-Based Syst. **23**(5), 440–454 (2010)
116. Oster, Z.J., Ali, S.A., Santhanam, G.R., Basu, S., Roop, P.S.: A service composition framework based on goal-oriented requirements engineering, model checking, and qualitative preference analysis. In: Service-Oriented Computing, pp. 283–297. Springer, Heidelberg (2012)
117. Oster, Z.J., Santhanam, G.R., Basu, S.: Identifying optimal composite services by decomposing the service composition problem. In: Proceedings of the International Conference on Web Services, pp. 267–274. IEEE (2011)
118. Ozorhan, E.K., Kuban, E.K., Cicekli, N.K.: Automated composition of web services with the abductive event calculus. Inf. Sci. **180**(19), 3589–3613 (2010)
119. Peer, J.: A pddl based tool for automatic web service composition. In: Principles and Practice of Semantic Web Reasoning, pp. 149–163. Springer, Heidelberg (2004)
120. Peer, J.: Web service composition as ai planning-a survey (2005)
121. Pistore, M., Marconi, A., Bertoli, P., Traverso, P.: Automated composition of web services by planning at the knowledge level. In: Proceedings of the International Joint Conference on Artificial Intelligence, pp. 1252–1259 (2005)

122. Pistore, M., Traverso, P., Bertoli, P.: Automated composition of web services by planning in asynchronous domains. ICAPS **5**, 2–11 (2005)
123. Pistore, M., Traverso, P., Bertoli, P., Marconi, A.: Automated synthesis of composite bpel4ws web services. In: Proceedings of the International Conference on Web Services, pp. 293–301. IEEE (2005)
124. Ponnekanti, S.R., Fox, A.: Sword: A developer toolkit for web service composition. In: Proceedings of the Eleventh International World Wide Web Conference, Honolulu, HI, vol. 45 (2002)
125. Pu, K., Hristidis, V., Koudas, N.: Syntactic rule based approach to web service composition. In: Proceedings of the International Conference on Data Engineering, pp. 31–31. IEEE (2006)
126. Rahmani, H., GhasemSani, G., Abolhassani, H.: Automatic web service composition considering user non-functional preferences. In: Proceedings of the International Conference on Next Generation Web Services Practices, pp. 33–38. IEEE (2008)
127. Rao, J., Küngas, P.: Application of linear logic to web service composition. In: Proceedings of the International Conference on Web Services, Las Vegas, pp. 3–9. CSREA Press (2003)
128. Rao, J., Kungas, P., Matskin, M.: Logic-based web services composition: From service description to process model. In: Proceedings of the International Conference on Web Services, pp. 446–453. IEEE (2004)
129. Rao, J., Küngas, P., Matskin, M.: Composition of semantic web services using linear logic theorem proving. Inf. Syst. **31**(4), 340–360 (2006)
130. Rao, J., Su, X.: A survey of automated web service composition methods. In: Semantic Web Services and Web Process Composition, pp. 43–54. Springer, Heidelberg (2005)
131. Rich, C., Waters, R.C.: Automatic programming: myths and prospects. IEEE Comput. **21**(8), 40–51 (1988)
132. Rodriguez-Mier, P., Mucientes, M., Lama, M.: Automatic web service composition with a heuristic-based search algorithm. In: Proceedings of the International Conference on Web Services, pp. 81–88. IEEE (2011)
133. Rodriguez-Mier, P., Mucientes, M., Lama, M., Couto, M.I.: Composition of web services through genetic programming. Evol. Intell. **3**(3–4), 171–186 (2010)
134. Schuller, D., Eckert, J., Miede, A., Schulte, S., Steinmetz, R.: Qos-aware service composition for complex workflows. In: Proceedings of the International Conference on Internet, Web Applications and Services, pp. 333–338. IEEE (2010)
135. Sheshagiri, M., DesJardins, M., Finin, T.: A planner for composing services described in daml-s. Web Serv. Agent-based Eng.-AAMAS **3**, 1–5 (2003)
136. Sirbu, A., Hoffmann, J.: Towards scalable web service composition with partial matches. In: Proceedings of the International Conference on Web Services, pp. 29–36. IEEE (2008)
137. Sirin, E., Parsia, B., Hendler, J.: Template-based composition of semantic web services. In: AAAI Fall Symposium on Agents and the Semantic Web, vol. 5, p. 01. AAAI (2005)
138. Sirin, E., Parsia, B., Wu, D., Hendler, J., Nau, D.: HTN planning for web service composition using SHOP2. Web Semant.: Sci., Serv. Agents World Wide Web **1**(4), 377–396 (2004)
139. Sivashanmugam, K., Miller, J.A., Sheth, A.P., Verma, K.: Framework for semantic web process composition. Int. J. Electron. Commer. **9**(2), 71–106 (2005)
140. Sohrabi, S., Prokoshyna, N., McIlraith, S.A.: Web service composition via generic procedures and customizing user preferences. In: The Semantic Web-ISWC 2006, pp. 597–611. Springer, Heidelberg (2006)
141. Sohrabi, S., Prokoshyna, N., McIlraith, S.A.: Web service composition via the customization of golog programs with user preferences. In: Conceptual Modeling: Foundations and Applications, pp. 319–334. Springer, Heidelberg (2009)
142. Srivastava, B., Koehler, J.: Web service composition-current solutions and open problems. In: ICAPS 2003 workshop on Planning for Web Services, vol. 35, pp. 28–35 (2003)
143. Srivastava, S., Gulwani, S., Foster, J.S.: From program verification to program synthesis. ACM Sigplan Not. **45**(1), 313–326 (2010)
144. Stickel, M., Waldinger, R., Lowry, M., Pressburger, T., Underwood, I.: Deductive composition of astronomical software from subroutine libraries. In: Automated Deduction—CADE-12, pp. 341–355. Springer, Heidelberg (1994)

145. Sun, P.: Service composition and optimal selection with trust constraints. In: Proceedings of the Asia-Pacific Services Computing Conference, pp. 645–653. IEEE (2010)
146. Sun, S.X., Zhao, J.: A decomposition-based approach for service composition with global qos guarantees. Inf. Sci. **199**, 138–153 (2012)
147. Syu, Y., Ma, S.P., Kuo, J.Y., FanJiang, Y.Y.: A survey on automated service composition methods and related techniques. In: Proceedings of the International Conference on Services Computing, pp. 290–297. IEEE (2012)
148. Talantikite, H.N., Aissani, D., Boudjlida, N.: Semantic annotations for web services discovery and composition. Comput. Stand. Interfaces **31**(6), 1108–1117 (2009)
149. Thakkar, S., Knoblock, C.A., Ambite, J.L., Shahabi, C.: Dynamically composing web services from on-line sources. In: Proceedings of the AAAI-2002 Workshop on Intelligent Service Integration, pp. 1–7 (2002)
150. Thiagarajan, R., Stumptner, M.: Service composition with consistency-based matchmaking: a csp-based approach. In: Proceedings of the European Conference on Web Services, pp. 23–32. IEEE (2007)
151. Traverso, P., Pistore, M.: Automated composition of semantic web services into executable processes. In: The Semantic Web, pp. 380–394. Springer, Heidelberg (2004)
152. Vallée, M., Ramparany, F., Vercouter, L.: Flexible composition of smart device services. PSC **5**, 165–171 (2005)
153. Verma, K.: Configuration and adaptation of semantic web processes. Ph.D. thesis, University of Georgia (2006)
154. Verma, K., Akkiraju, R., Goodwin, R., Doshi, P., Lee, J.: On accommodating inter service dependencies in web process flow composition. In: AAAI spring symposium on semantic web services, pp. 37–43 (2004)
155. Verma, K., Doshi, P., Gomadam, K., Miller, J., Sheth, A.: Optimal adaptation in web processes with coordination constraints. In: Proceedings of the International Conference on Web Services, pp. 257–264. IEEE (2006)
156. Verma, K., Gomadam, K., Sheth, A.P., Miller, J., Wu, Z.: The METEOR-S approach for configuring and executing dynamic web processes (2005)
157. Vuković, M., Kotsovinos, E., Robinson, P.: An architecture for rapid, on-demand service composition. Serv. Oriented Comput. Appl. **1**(4), 197–212 (2007)
158. Wada, H., Suzuki, J., Yamano, Y.: Oba, K.: E&# xb3;: A multiobjective optimization framework for sla-aware service composition. Trans. Serv. Comput. **5**(3), 358–372 (2012)
159. Wagner, F.: Efficient, failure-resilient semantic web service planning. In: Service-Oriented Computing, pp. 686–689. Springer, Heidelberg (2010)
160. Wagner, F., Ishikawa, F., Honiden, S.: Qos-aware automatic service composition by applying functional clustering. In: Proceedings of the International Conference on Web Services, pp. 89–96. IEEE (2011)
161. Weise, T., Bleul, S., Comes, D., Geihs, K.: Different approaches to semantic web service composition. In: Proceedings of the International Conference on Internet and Web Applications and Services, pp. 90–96. IEEE (2008)
162. Wu, B., Deng, S., Li, Y., Wu, J., Yin, J.: Awsp: an automatic web service planner based on heuristic state space search. In: Proceedings of the International Conference on Web Services, pp. 403–410. IEEE (2011)
163. Wu, D., Parsia, B., Sirin, E., Hendler, J., Nau, D.: Automating DAML-S Web Services Composition Using SHOP2. Springer, Heidelberg (2003)
164. Xu, J., Reiff-Marganiec, S.: Towards heuristic web services composition using immune algorithm. In: Proceedings of the International Conference on Web Services, pp. 238–245. IEEE (2008)
165. Yan, Y., Chen, M., Yang, Y.: Anytime qos optimization over the plangraph for web service composition. In: Proceedings of the 27th Annual ACM Symposium on Applied Computing, pp. 1968–1975. ACM (2012)
166. Yan, Y., Poizat, P., Zhao, L.: Self-adaptive service composition through graph plan repair. In: Proceedings of the International Conference on Web Services, pp. 624–627. IEEE (2010)

167. Zeng, L., Benatallah, B., Dumas, M., Kalagnanam, J., Sheng, Q.Z.: Quality driven web services composition. In: Proceedings of the 12th International Conference on World Wide Web, pp. 411–421. ACM (2003)
168. Zeng, L., Benatallah, B., Ngu, A.H., Dumas, M., Kalagnanam, J., Chang, H.: Qos-aware middleware for web services composition. IEEE Trans. Softw. Eng. **30**(5), 311–327 (2004)
169. Zeng, L., Ngu, A.H., Benatallah, B., Podorozhny, R., Lei, H.: Dynamic composition and optimization of web services. Distrib. Parallel Databases **24**(1–3), 45–72 (2008)
170. Zhou, A., Huang, S., Wang, X.: Bits: a binary tree based web service composition system. Int. J. Web Serv. Res. **4**(1), 40 (2007)
171. Zou, G., Gan, Y., Chen, Y., Zhang, B.: Dynamic composition of web services using efficient planners in large-scale service repository. Knowl.-Based Syst. **62**, 98–112 (2014)
172. Zou, G., Lu, Q., Chen, Y., Huang, R., Xu, Y., Xiang, Y.: Qos-aware dynamic composition of web services using numerical temporal planning. Trans. Serv. Comput. **7**(1), 18–31 (2014)

Printed in the United States
By Bookmasters